Don't eat
while reading

Everyday Armageddons

Everyday Armageddons

Stories and Reflections on Death, Dying, God, and Waste

MATTHEW HOLMES
and THOMAS R. GAULKE

Foreword by Cláudio Carvalhaes

CASCADE *Books* • Eugene, Oregon

EVERYDAY ARMAGEDDONS
Stories and Reflections on Death, Dying, God, and Waste

Cascade Books
An Imprint of Wipf and Stock Publishers
199 W. 8th Ave., Suite 3
Eugene, OR 97401

www.wipfandstock.com

PAPERBACK ISBN: 978-1-6667-6509-0
HARDCOVER ISBN: 978-1-6667-6510-6
EBOOK ISBN: 978-1-6667-6511-3

Cataloguing-in-Publication data:

Names: Holmes, Matthew, author. | Gaulke, Thomas R., author. | Carvalhaes,
Cláudio, foreword.

Title: Everyday armageddons : stories and reflections on death, dying, god,
and waste / Matthew Holmes and Thomas R. Gaulke ; foreword by Cláudio
Carvalhaes.

Description: Eugene, OR : Cascade Books, 2023 | Includes bibliographical
references.

Identifiers: ISBN 978-1-6667-6509-0 (paperback) | ISBN 978-1-6667-6510-6
(hardcover) | ISBN 978-1-6667-6511-3 (ebook)

Subjects: LCSH: Terminal care. | Death.

Classification: R726.8 .H65 2023 (paperback) | R726.8 .H65 (ebook)

11/12/23

To my Grandma Nancy who showed me to live in a way that drove everyone nuts, and to die the way she wanted.

~ Matt

To Dolores, her prayers, and her dancing—and to every faith community that is also a family for those who find themselves without one.

~ Tom

Contents

List of Illustrations

Cover artwork, electronic imaging by Thomas R. Gaulke using: Say, Frederick Richard. *A diseased brain.* 1829, colored aquatint. Wellcome Collection, London. Reference: 30957i, Public Domain.

Chapter 1, Bosch, Hieronymus. *Death of a Miser.* 1450–1516, painting. Samuel H. Kress Collection, National Gallery of Art, Washington DC. Public Domain. Accession number 1952.5.33

Chapter 2, Godart, Thomas. *Acute Synovitis of the Knee Joint.* 1872, watercolor drawing. Wellcome Collection, London. License: Attribution 4.0 International (CC BY 4.0).

Chapter 3, *Burial of Christ.* Ca. 1900, folding icon. Ethiopian Collection, SMA African Art Museum, Tenafly, New Jersey (photo: Victoria Emily Jones). Icon: Public Domain. Photograph used with photographer's permission.

Chapter 4, Danielssen, Daniel Cornelius; Losting, Johan Ludvig; and Boeck, Wilhelm. *Tubercular leprosy on the hand.* From *Om spedalskhed . . . Atlas / udgivet efter foranstaltning of den Kongelige Norske Regjerings Department for det Indre. Tegningerne udförte af J.L. Losting.* 1847, colored drawing. Wellcome Collection, London. License: Attribution 4.0 International (CC BY 4.0).

Chapter 5, Kusōzu. *The Death of a Noble Lady and the Decay of her Body.* 1700–1799, watercolors. Wellcome Collection, London. License: Attribution 4.0 International (CC BY 4.0).

Chapter 6, Kahlo, Frida. *El Sueño (La Cama).* 1940, oil on canvas. Nesuhi Ertegun Collection, New York City. License: Attribution 4.0 International (CC BY 4.0).

Chapter 7, Fairland, William (after Walsh, J). *The Aorta and Ribs.* 1837, colored lithograph. Wellcome Collection, London. License: Attribution 4.0 International (CC BY 4.0).

Chapter 8, *A Man, Half Human and Half Skeleton.* Unknown date, etching. London (No. 69 in St. Paul's churchyard): printed for & sold by Bowles & Carver. Wellcome Collection, London. License: Attribution 4.0 International (CC BY 4.0).

Foreword

by Cláudio Carvalhaes

Death is a mystery; and oftentimes none of us want to think about the way in which we die. The final months, days, hours, minutes of our existence are moments we can't really predict. They can be careless, miserable, frustrating, even shocking. They can be beautiful, expensive, underfunded, isolating, heart-wrenching, disorienting, confusing, unknown. But they can also be a celebration, a moment filled with joy and gratitude, a love unknown fully lived.

The writers of this book engage with these last moments of life. Matthew Holmes narrates the end of lives of people from different social realities. In every story, the fullness of the body in all its dazzling, strange, fantastic movements. The ways of the body, the smells, the weight, the skin, the wounds, the conditions of treatment, and the sure presence of death. The absurd hovers around. The word absurd from Latin means *ab-surdus*: a noise so loud that it makes us deaf. In every story a quiet but deafening sound of death in its process and its final fullness. How can we make sense of that which doesn't seem to give itself to our Western Christian senses? This is the work of Thomas Gaulke who responds to the absurd with broken theologies, fractal ways of sense, half-thoughts, comedy, poetry, cognitive dissonance, and imaginative connections.

In the book *The Myth of Sisyphus*, Albert Camus says that there is only one question to ask: "There is only one really serious philosophical question, and that is suicide."[1] When we read the stories of people bound to bed and "assisted" in nursing homes and assisted living in this book, this question pulses mightily in front of our eyes. For those not used to these facilities, it

1. Camus, *Myth of Sisyphus*, 5–7.

is shocking to hear about the abandonment, the struggle of the employees, and the total lack of care of the elderly. In most stories, so much pain and hurt could have been avoided, and even death could have been more honorable. Matthew Holmes writes these stories with a mixture of a matter-of-fact spirit, as well as a huge frustration and anger for what he sees happening. His love for these people is also everywhere in these stories. Perhaps the only way to write about the sadness of it all is to show the shocking aspects of the ways the lives of people without resources are treated.

These stories are not new to me. My wife, Katie, is a home health and hospice occupational therapist and she tells me these stories weekly. I ask her if there is a way out and she says: if you have financial resources, a supportive family who is knowledgeable about navigating our health care systems, and strong pastoral care or faith community, you have the potential to have very good care. Then she tells me that the best way to care for someone is at home when you have a family that deeply cares for you and has the capacity, means, and will to care for their dying loved ones. She also knows this subject personally, as she cared for her first husband, Peter, who died from a rare and aggressive sinus cancer at thirty-five years old.

These stories make us ask for the quest of assisted suicide, which I am in favor of and hope to make use of if I am bedbound. But these are questions we all need to ask as we think about our own stories. The very narrations of these stories already carry a worldview, a psychological perspective and theological positionalities. Thus, both writers are very clear in their perspective of life and death, God and faith. It belongs to the reader to agree or not and actually see what life, death, and God might mean to them.

This book made me consider the notion of death again. While I am educated in death as absurd, threat, contention, abandonment, shatter of meaning, disaster, and something that should never happen, I have never truly learned with Saint Francis to call death my Sister Death.[2] What is bringing me close to Saint Francis is Buddhism. I have learned with Buddhist friends that death is just another moment of life. Moreover, one never dies, they say. My brother and sensei Greg Snyder reminded me of the "Five Remembrances" in Buddhism:

1. I am of the nature to grow old. There is no way to escape growing old.

2. I am of the nature to have ill health. There is no way to escape having ill health.

2. Francis of Assisi, "Canticle of the Creatures," 114.

3. I am of the nature to die. There is no way to escape death.

4. All that is dear to me and everyone I love are of the nature to change. There is no way to escape being separated from them.

5. My actions are my only true belongings. I cannot escape the consequences of my actions. My actions are the ground upon which I stand.[3]

This perspective changes everything in my way of thinking about death and consequently life. As a pastor, I officiated several funerals and some of them were absolutely painful, desperate, and horrific. On the other hand, the memories of death I have from beloved ones are all beautiful: I remember my mother telling us about the way her mother died. She was nine years old. One night, her mother, Maria Dias, came to put her to bed and said, "My daughter, tonight mom will go live with God forever." My grandmother was extremely sick and couldn't hold it any longer. My mom also remembers the way her father-in-law died. José was already in a very frail situation and she was his caretaker. One morning when she opened the window of his room, he lifted up his back and looked up and said, "The angel . . . the angel . . ." and fell to the bed dead. And the way my father Waldemar died was also so beautiful. He was seventy-five and one night he felt sick. The neighbor put him in the back seat of the car with my mom to take them to the hospital. He rested his head on her shoulder, held her hand, and on the way to the hospital he had a heart attack and died.

There is something to the fact that if one can have songs, prayers, and a community of love and sustenance, that changes everything. If Christians took their baptismal vow seriously, they would never let go of their beloved ones if they were sick, even sick unto death. For a baptismal vow demands us to hold each other's hands all the way to the very last breath of life and then, only then, give the person to God. But we have so much to do, we are so annoyed by the elderly and the sick that we can't find much time to care for them.

This book is a gift in that way: it gives us the possibility to think about ourselves in relation to the elderly, to the diseased, and makes us think about who we are and what makes us who we are. It makes us check our beliefs but it sends us way beyond that, it makes us see what life and death are all about.

With this gift, this book takes us within ourselves and into places we do not expect. It offers ways of getting closer to those who died while no

---

3. Franz, "Buddhism's 'Five Remembrances,'" para. 2.

one watched or cared. This book offers us a chance to be witnesses to the bound, limited, and lost bodies of these unknown people. The book lays bare the conditions of our limitations in the last moments of our lives. The book asks deep theological questions, pushing us beyond the systematization sought in so many books and creeds. The authors make us ponder deeply about these moments, challenging the loneliness facilitated by our fractured societal systems and systems of health. They make us look for ways to connect with something that might help us bring honor to the last moments of the diseased. And perhaps in the end that is the point. To cultivate a sense of caring for those who are vulnerable is to prepare ourselves to face the inevitability of our own death in whatever way it may come.

Preface

by Matthew Holmes

"She's suffered enough." Work with the dying and this is a phrase that will become so common it will bounce off of you. The same as someone saying, "How're you doing?" when passing you on the street. A pleasantry, it is a statement made without thought, simply because the situation seems to call for it. Somebody has died. Something must be said. "She's suffered enough," fits the bill. It goes with the territory. But what happens if we step back for a moment? What if we were to look at this sentiment and its assumptions with fresh eyes? What do we mean, and what are we really saying when we say to one another, "She's suffered enough?"

This is the question that sparked this book, bringing pen to paper and expanding into all that is contained hereafter. What do we mean when we say, "she's suffered enough"? While concrete answers to this question may be satisfying, stories tend to offer us something truer. And so, what follows are stories. After all, in the end, death is at the bottom of everything.

At the same time, these stories, like any death, are also shot through with life and love—with humor and strength, struggle and acceptance. Between these stories are theopoetic interludes—breaks in the narrative to sit back, listen, and reflect. Time to allow for meaning to make its way in.

The stories are works of fiction. However, they are also born from years of experience working with the dying and the dead. Any of them could happen on any given day in any hospital room, living room, or dying room. These stories are not meant to be easy to read. At times, they may seem playful or fun, but they are not that alone. Rather, they are honest and they speak of what is happening all around us and inside us, every moment of our existence.

I work in death, it's my business, but it's your business, too. The stories in this book will one day be your story, the story of your parents, your partner, your children. There may be other stories to write, better ones, but if we can't read stories like these together, the narrative will remain as it is.

There are points in the following text that may appear critical of the medical industry and the people who work in it. The critique of the system is, in places, intentional. Any critique of individual characters that appear, however, is meant not to cast them in a negative light, but rather to highlight the problems with the whole. The fact of the matter is, after two decades in health care I can truly say that some of the greatest people I have known work in the medical field. It draws empathic, bright, and kind people. Unfortunately, it also places too much on those people. Any failures featured herein are of the industry, not the individual.

In the past hundred years, the average American lifespan has increased by nearly three decades. While a good thing, this extra time has also created the conditions for modern, ordinary death—death marked by chronic illness, lengthy pervasive debility, and often isolation from community. Most of us, most of our friends and family, and most of the world will die an ordinary, modern death. Our deaths will not make the news. They will not be discussed by strangers. They won't be written about by generations to come. Rather, they will happen behind closed doors, tucked away from the world, after a lengthy period of pain, illness, and cognitive decline. *Everyday Armageddons: Stories and Reflections on Death, Dying, God, and Waste* is a collection of narratives, stories, and theopoetic reflections about those ordinary deaths.

Modern death is a new phenomenon attached to the oldest. It presents new and unique challenges, but the same love, care, and loss. The same horror and healing, courage and fear, darkness and light sit shoulder to shoulder at the bedside. If you read on, you can take your place with them, and maybe start to find your way through them.

Thank You,
Matt Holmes

CHAPTER ONE

Jeffrey Goes to Assisted Living

Jeffrey was an old man when he arrived at Joyful Days Assisted Living Facility. When Jeff's son and daughter-in-law had toured the facility a few days prior, when they walked through the double doors into the atrium, all they smelled was buttered popcorn. It smelled more like buttered popcorn than a movie theater, more than when your mom made Jiffy Pop on movie night, more like buttered popcorn than Orville Redenbacher's living room. Don't eat the buttered popcorn at an assisted living facility; it is not food. It is a kind of potpourri meant to cover up the eye-watering scent of aging feces and dried piss that filled the diapers of the patients who the staff had been kind enough to park for the day near the front door of the facility.

The front desk worker got Jeff's family a paper plate of popcorn, and they ate it. They didn't eat it because they were hungry but because what else is someone to do with a paper plate of popcorn while they wait for the sales staff of an assisted living facility? The front desk worker, a high school girl with the blonde hair and blue eyes of the neighborhood, as opposed to the dark skin and brown eyes of the rest of the staff who came from other places, didn't think much of handing them the popcorn. She didn't even consider the fact that Sally, one of the residents with a heavy diaper and a severe case of Methicillin-resistant Staphylococcus aureus (MRSA) had just been digging around in the popcorn machine with her bare unwashed hands. Sally wasn't hungry, she just enjoyed the feeling of the warm popcorn on her paper-thin skin.

Maybe Jeff's son should have been more aware, but his mind was taken up with his father. Jeffrey had Alzheimer's. He forgot when to go to the john, he had forgotten how to put on his clothing properly, and had gotten really angry, even belligerent, with them on occasion. This was a real pain in the ass, and as such an assisted living facility was now the safest place for Jeff. This one looked nice enough on the outside to allow Jeff's son to feel comfortable leaving the old man there. It couldn't be any worse than the POW camp Jeff had spent time in during the war. Even if the view wasn't as nice as the Singapore beach, the faux Victorian mansion of Joyful Days Assisted Living had its own Stepford wife prefabricated luxury aesthetic.

Jeffrey's son Mike and his wife sat munching the popcorn and waiting. The salesperson didn't really have to rush. Does the day care center or the public school really need to sell themselves, or do they just have to be in the right place at the right cost? Eventually, she came out. The salesperson, known as a "neighborhood welcomer" didn't look like the high school kid at the front desk, nor did she look like the various staff doing patient care. She was a bubbly woman, in her early thirties, with short brown not unstylish hair. She wore a smart pantsuit, also not unstylish. She was late because all afternoon she had been working on her wedding, the date was mid-June. Her last day at Joyful Days would be July first, the honeymoon would take up the two weeks in between.

"Hello, I'm Karen. Welcome to our little community here. I see you already got some of our popcorn. Keep it away from me; I'm getting married in two months and need to fit into my dress." Karen made a little cross with her fingers and a big smile with her lips. Pleasantries being over, Karen took Mike and his wife, also named Karen, on the tour. It wasn't a long tour, the place was only so big. Two floors with four wings met at a central hub where the front desk was located on the first floor and the nurses' station on the second. The floors were carpeted, the walls papered. It didn't have the institutional feel of a usual nursing home, or at least it tried to pretend it didn't. Karen, the salesperson and not the daughter-in-law, pointed this out, neglecting to say they weren't required to have infection control and safety measures like washable floors and handrails on the wall because they didn't take filthy government money with all its strings attached. That also meant their staff had no real training outside of a two-day course, which consisted of mostly anti-union and sexual harassment videos. One to save money, one as the result of a lawsuit in which they paid handsomely.

They walked the hallways. Karen took them into the "tub room" to show Mike the beautiful spa-like "hydro-tub" Jeffrey could luxuriate in for hours. They were only in the room for a minute before Karen ushered them out and shut the door. Karen hoped they didn't have time to notice the mound of human waste that sat uncleaned in the bottom of the hydro-tub from the shift before. Karen kicked herself; she knew better than to show them the tub room. The picture in the brochure never had human waste in it. She made a mental note not to show them any of the public restrooms. Jeffrey's family didn't seem to, or didn't want to, notice anything.

The model room was next. A standard double room, they only put one bed in the model, making it look bigger. Karen mentioned Jeff would have a roommate, but nobody asked about how they would fit. The room was clean and smelled nice except for when they went into the bathroom where Maggie, one of the "care specialists" who did most of the hands-on caregiving, was enjoying her five-minute break on the toilet. Again, the family didn't seem to notice. After the tour, Karen took them back to her office. It smelled of popcorn.

Jeffrey's family got settled in the office while Karen grabbed a couple of six-ounce Cokes from the kitchen as well as a piece of chocolate cake. The cake was good at Joyful Days Assisted Living. They had an arrangement with an industrial pastry company to make them thousands of these delicious cakes a week. They were shipped all around the country, to every "community" they owned. It might seem expensive, but there was a logic. The number one complaint of nursing home and assisted living residents is the food, because it's awful. Joyful Days realized that if the families were given a delicious treat, a slice of chocolate cake, this would stick with them so that when the resident complained later the family could always remind them of the delicious cake they ate when they were visiting. The cake is not as good blended up into a mush, wetted down with thickened water, and fed to a person with a spoon as is usually the case at Joyful Days. That is, if a "care specialist" actually has the time to do the feeding.

Once Karen had Jeffrey's family enjoying their treat, she flipped on the flat screen hanging on the wall behind her desk. "This is a little welcome video that our owners like everyone to see." She hit play. A blue sky dotted with fluffy little clouds appeared on the screen. Music, something like what you might expect to hear at an Evangelical Church or a funeral home, began to play gently. *Joyful Days Assisted Living Communities* appeared among the clouds in gold lettering just as a dove flew across the perfect sky. The scene then cut to a man and woman sitting in front of a fireplace. They sat in giant plush pink chairs that had six-feet-tall backs. The man wore a blue suit and a non-threatening pink tie. He was in his fifties or sixties and appeared to be in good health. The woman was blonde, with a puff of thin hair teased almost to the top of the chair. She wore a white dress like an angel, or a very socially inept person at a wedding. You didn't have to hear them speak to know they'd have southern accents.

"Hello, I'm Owsley Grace and this is my wife Nancy." This was all that Owsley would say for the video, though his gaze would say, "I'm trying my best to look like I care, but really I just want to take all your money." Owsley was the star and narrator of all the anti-union videos they made new hires watch during orientation.

"You know when we first started Joyful Days Assisted Living, we did it out of love. Our lives have been driven by a deep passion to care for our seniors, to offer them a place to call home. At Joyful Days we believe the last chapter of life can be the best chapter of life. From our award-winning dining [the award was given by, paid for, and voted on by the board members of Joyful Days LLC], to our selection of books in our library [the books in the library were made up entirely of books left behind when residents died. A surprising amount of questionable military history and knot-tying manuals], your loved one will find a life of relaxation and comfort in our communities."

"We at Joyful Days provide excellent programing." Images appeared on the screen of speakers giving talks, preachers preaching sermons, old people doing the limbo at a community luau. What the pictures didn't show was the audience of wheelchair dependent, slumped over, sleeping and drooling "residents."

"From our spa-like amenities to our world class nursing care." By "world class" they mean a licensed practical nurse who is present between 9 a.m. and 5 p.m. Monday through Friday. The rest of the time the nursing care was done by the untrained "care specialists" making slightly under minimum wage for extremely demanding work. The nursing care was done by "care specialists" and 911, whose services they regularly called. "We at Joyful Days know that you want the best for your loved one, and that's what we provide. You can confidently entrust your loved one's care to us, because care is what we are all about here at Joyful Days."

That was it; Jeff's family was sold. It's hard to say if it was Karen's sales pitch, the aesthetic charm of the facility, Nancy Grace's mountain of hair and piercingly blue, dead, yet somehow dangerous eyes. Could have been none of those or all, but mostly it was the filth they had to wash out of Jeffrey's shorts that morning. Either way, within the week Jeffrey left behind everything he had and everything he knew to come to this new home.

Now one might think that with a progressive dementia like Alzheimer's it would be easy to move to a new place. After all, if you can't remember your surroundings, what does it matter if those surroundings change? This isn't the case in reality. What we can recall is one thing, what we can remember is another. We remember colors, shapes, smells. Our bodies remember what the air in a house feels like, our souls remember the love shared in that place, the times past. A person with advanced dementia might not be able to tell you their name, but move them out of a familiar place and put them someplace new, and they will notice.

When Jeffrey arrived at the facility, he could still stand on his own. He could follow some direction. If you held his hand, you could lead Jeffrey from the bedroom to the bathroom, even down the hall to the dining room. This made Jeffrey easy to take care of early in the day; the problems began after dark when he would experience what is known as "sundowning."

It has something to do with circadian rhythms, or maybe just the rhythm of life in the modern world, but rhythm is definitely involved. When the day grew long, Jeffrey would get wild. Maybe the staff could have done a better job of keeping him up during the day, taking him to the various activities they claimed the people loved so much, but Jeffrey seemed perfectly happy dozing in his chair. Since he was happy, they left him there in his room, one less person to keep an eye on was a good thing for the afternoon staff. During the day Jeffrey caught his Zs, a bother to nobody, but he was up and goofy all night.

Jeffrey would get up from his chair and wander. First, it was in his apartment. He tried doors and opened windows. He ran the water in the bathroom and flushed the toilet. Often he would be found out by the nurses' station, in the laundry room opening doors on the washers, pushing the buttons on the drier. One night, Jeff got out. By the grace of God, a "care specialist" taking their break at the McDonald's next door caught him wandering in the drive through.

The sundowning was a problem. It became a crisis when Jeffrey, while wandering, climbed into bed with his roommate. The roommate was further along in his dementia than Jeffrey and had not been out of bed in well over a year, and not spoken a word in longer. That said, he still could shout, and the scared and confused man shouted and shouted. This spooked Jeffrey who fell out of the bed and onto the ground. Jeffrey was left with a large skin tear on his leg. Skin tears are common for older folks as their flesh can become thin and fragile. Jeffrey's roommate was inconsolable. A person can lose the ability to talk, to walk, to sing and dance, but they can still fear. Nothing could calm Jeff's roommate until the next morning when the nurse came in with some Haldol. Haldol is an antipsychotic that chemically lobotomized the roommate for a while. The staff knew Haldol as vitamin H.

What is good for the goose is good for the gander. From this day forward not only was Jeffrey's roommate on vitamin H but so was Jeffrey himself. The facility told the family that it would help with the sundowning and let Jeffrey sleep. The rounding doctor who spent a total of one whole minute and a half with Jeffrey said it was "absolutely necessary" if Jeffrey was to remain under his care. He could not "in good conscience" let Jeffrey put himself and others at risk in the middle of the night. Jeff's family didn't want anyone to be at risk, and couldn't fathom Jeffrey being evicted from the facility. After the addition of vitamin H and a number of other drugs, all meant to help Jeffrey with those aspects of his illness that made him a "little bit much" for staff and residents to deal with, Jeffrey stayed in bed. It made him harder to take care of in some respects and easier in others. The easier outweighed the harder.

It was easy to walk him over to the bathroom, pull down his diaper and sit him on the john, but easier still to just change him in bed most of the time. Sometimes though, Jeffrey would find the strength to latch onto the handrail mid-changing. When that happened, changing Jeffrey would take two people: one to pry his hand off the rail and another to do the actual changing. While this may have been physically more demanding than walking Jeffrey to the bathroom, it took a quarter of the time and time is money.

At this point, all Jeffrey did during the day was lay and sit. Sitting in dirty diapers is like sitting in battery acid, and so over time Jeffrey's skin began to break down. Wounds formed and grew infected. He was put on new medications for the wounds, all of which took a toll on his body. Jeffrey, who showed up physically capable though mentally declining, fell off a cliff, as it were. He went from mobile and pleasant to bedbound and comatose. Jeffrey was still strong. His powerful hands were the bane of existence for the staff paid to take care of him, but even they weakened, some on their own and some due to vitamin H. Eventually he stopped grabbing the bed rails. Once in a while, even up to the end, he would get a hold of a staff member's hand and squeeze as hard as he could. It didn't really hurt, but some staff members would complain and the drugs would be upped.

Being stuck in bed, full of holes, unable to talk or eat or fend for yourself, beats a body down. His breath became agonal, meaning there were large gaps between each respiration. Over and over again it appeared as if he had taken his last breath, only for him to gasp once more. It went on like this for weeks. His kids came and stayed with him when they could. The first couple days of this "actively dying" phase they were there round the clock, but it dragged on and who could stand to stay at Joyful Days around the clock? Eventually they were just stopping by for an hour or two a day, and then less. If it goes on long enough, even active death can be gotten used to. After the first few weeks, Jeff's family went back to their weekly drop-in schedule they had kept since Jeffrey arrived.

If you asked them and were able to get a real answer out of them, Jeffrey's family might have said they were tired of the emotional roller coaster; the constant knife's edge of "will this be his last day or not, last breath or not?" This would be true, but they also were tired of having to stop off after work, and nervous that they might have to stay home from the vacation they had planned in two weeks. That vacation had been on their books for months. Eventually, they brought in hospice care, but it really didn't change the situation all that much. Jeffrey still spent his days in bed, vacillating between resting peacefully while medicated or pulling on his clothes, reaching out at nothing when not. Hospice did up the dosage of some of his medicine, but the staff at the Joyful Days were nervous to give the higher dosage, and so they didn't. Nobody wanted to be responsible for hastening Jeffrey's death. Of course, one might blame the dementia for that, or his age, or the fact he hadn't truly consumed any food or liquid in weeks now—just a few wet sponges pressed between his lips.

Jeffrey's daughter sat by the bedside one night. She had heard that she needed to give her dad permission to "go." Wherever he was "going to" wasn't clear. She struggled to do it, this was her dad after all, and like the staff, she didn't want to bear responsibility for his death. Eventually though, watching her father in his state of living death, she gave in. She said, "Dad, we are okay, you gave us what we need to survive. You can go now." She knew they weren't magic words, she knew he wouldn't just die right when the sound reached his ears. Still, it was so hard to say the words and it seemed like something should have happened then and there. It was a bit of a let down when nothing changed.

Nothing happened. It doesn't really mean "nothing" happened. Jeffrey slept. He gasped. His throat rang out the "death rattle" that happens when an esophagus no longer has the muscle strength to clear phlegm. The mucus pools in the back of the throat and just kind of flaps around with the breath, like a playing card attached to the spokes of a bike. The staff tried to suction the phlegm now and then but it only made Jeffrey gag. They stopped the suctioning and instead applied a patch with Scopolamine. Scopolamine dries secretions along with, according to some, creating zombies and helping with seasickness—a wonder drug.

Then the day came. Nothing seemed different. The family had been by, but they had just left. The family would speculate later that Jeffrey picked after they had left to die so they wouldn't have to see it. If he had died just as they arrived they would've said he chose that moment because he wanted them around. Who knows what volition we have in the day and hour of our death. What we do know is that it happened when the "care specialist" went to change Jeffrey's diaper. James was new to the job. He wasn't planning on staying a "care specialist" for long. James had a college degree and all, but there weren't a lot of people hiring at the time. He took this job because Joyful Days would hire a philosophy major with nothing else going on. It wasn't that a philosophy degree was important to Joyful Days, a body was important to Joyful Days and this kid had one of those.

James knew that Jeffrey was dying. He didn't mind much, but other members of the staff did. Staff got nervous when people began to "decline." Decline from where was never clear. Many of the other "care specialists" would do what they could to make sure that the dying patients were given to other staff, even picking up more work to avoid caring for the dying. James was fine with this; he didn't mind death nearly as much and he loved less work. As such, he was happy to take Jeffrey's case that day.

James walked up to Jeffrey gasping for air. Jeffrey's eyes were open, open in the specific and mechanical sense, but they saw nothing. Clouded over, Jeffrey's eyes were trained on the ceiling, perhaps through the ceiling. The eyes were dry and streaked with red. The stinging tears that had dripped down for days had dried up. If those tears had been a sign of fear or pain or sorrow or sadness, the horror would be too much. They were simply the product of not blinking. A person could only really live, with Jeffrey being alive in this condition, if they could assume that the person of Jeffrey had no idea what was happening to the body of Jeffrey.

"Hey Jeff," James called out. When James first started, the woman that trained him, a war refugee tougher than old horse jerky, had told him he needed to talk to the people he was taking care of. He needed to let them know what he was doing and what he was going to do on the off chance they could hear. James followed her orders as much out of fear of her as he did out of respect for Jeffrey.

"Okay Jeffrey, I'm going to change you now," James lifted the thin sheet off the man. The thin unnatural material of the sheet reached down to his feet but didn't cover them. There was a dirty comforter on a chair in the corner of the room. The morning shift had forgotten to remove and re-place the soiled linen. This was not uncommon. Under the sheet was white flesh, truly white to the point of transparency. Blue and green veins, like wires, worked their way just beneath and bulged through his flesh. It was as though Jeffrey was thinning out of existence, one layer at a time. James noticed a red spot on his ankle bone where the skin was starting to break down. A body ripping apart, simply from one leg sitting on the other. James thought about telling the nurse about it, but he knew she would get angry at him for making more work. She had too many charts to review to do something as menial as patient care. Plus, she had a book of crosswords that weren't going to solve themselves. The doctor had told the nurse she needed more mental stimulation.

James opened up a fresh diaper, he lined it up with the bone and loose skin that was Jeffrey's backside. He pushed down on the bed sliding some of the diaper under Jeffrey's body, as much of it as he could. Jeffrey, still laying and staring, seemed oblivious to what was going on. "Okay Jeffrey, I'm gonna take off the old diaper now." The kid undid the tabs and pulled the diaper down, exposing Jeffrey's penis. Just flesh now, no hair, no life. An exit point for piss that sometimes worked and often didn't. "I'm going to pull the old diaper out now." The kid pulled on the diaper, which slid out easily from under Jeffrey's body, leaving the new diaper still halfway lined up. As James did this, the door opened. Louise was standing on the threshold. James felt bad. Jeffrey was exposed and anybody who happened to be walking by could see his manhood plain as day.

"I need you to help me get Ruth in the tub. She shit all over herself," Louise said.

"Could you give me a minute? I'm kind of in the middle of something," James replied. Louise, who was a good worker and nice person came over to help the kid. "Ok Jeffrey, Louise is going to hold on to you while I slide the diaper under." James looked up at Louise.

"I don't know why you talk to him; he can't hear you."

"I don't know, Louise, can we just do this? One . . . two . . . three," James pushed Jeffrey up on his side, Louise held him in place. The kid wiped Jeffrey while Louise kept him upright. Once Jeff was reasonably clean, James shoved the diaper the rest of the way under his body. "Okay roll him back to me," James said, but Louise was frozen. She looked at James, big nervous eyes. He looked back at her, she looked down at Jeffrey, Jeffrey looked at nothing. He was gone. Life had drifted out as he was propped up on his side. This happens surprisingly often and is never an easy thing for the caregiver, unless said caregiver is a sociopath. Without thinking Louise let go of the body, which rolled back onto the bed. Already it moved differently than a living person, even a person as sick as Jeffrey was. It fell back like a ton of bricks, no reflex and no sound. James looked up at Louise, "What'd you do that for?"

"I didn't mean to," she looked scared and James felt bad.

"It's okay, not like he noticed." It wasn't a good time to joke, both because of the gravity of the situation and secondly because Jeffrey's daughter was now standing in the doorway. Neither James nor Louise knew what to say. James pulled the sheet over the lower half of the body, leaving the face exposed. People die in many different positions, but most of the time what happens to the face right after death is the jaw muscles loosen up. It seems we spend our living lives holding our jaws in place, but the second we shed the mortal coil, that task is shed as well. The mouth drops open with the effect being a body that looks like it's screaming. Couple that with the fact that the eyes are usually half open and a dead body can be a ghastly scene, especially for the family and the uninitiated.

Once the body was covered, both James and Louise turned and walked past the daughter. "I'm sorry Miss," Louise said, her eyes on the ground.

"We'll go and get the nurse," James whispered, terrified at how the nurse would react to being pulled from her paperwork to deal with something as time consuming as a death.

The next few hours were a delicate dance. Joyful Days wanted the body out immediately. This was for a number of reasons, but highest on that list was the roommate curled up in the bed next to Jeffrey's. Though the roommate lacked the faculties to raise a word of protest, still it was rude to just leave a dead body right next to a person who was halfway to the grave himself. On top of that, the management was worried that the roommate's family might stop by. They usually came on the weekends but had been known to pop in on random evenings once in a while.

The issue was that Jeffrey's family wanted to come and see Jeffrey. He was going to be cremated and had no desire to have a service of any kind. Jeffrey thought that funerals were just too "sad" and "expensive." As a way to save that expense, the family decided they would all come in to view Jeffrey's body before the cremation company arrived. It would take about an hour from notification for the family to get there. Knowing time was limited, the "manager on call" who was already five deep in at a Madonna impersonator concert and in no shape to show up in person, ordered James to get the body cleaned up.

James was clueless as to what a "cleaned up" corpse would look like. He asked Louise for help and while she was undeterred by colostomy bags, bed sores, full body diarrhea (both the normal way and from the mouth—this really happens and more often than you would think), the thought of touching dead flesh was too much for her or any of the other staff. James, who had never seen a dead body outside of his great grandma in a casket when he was ten years old, went back into the room.

James asked the daughter to please step outside, which she did without question. He then stripped the sheets off Jeffrey's body. It sat there exposed, only half clad in the diaper James had been putting on him. The kid had heard rumors and had seen on the TV that the human body expels every-thing from itself upon death and was worried about what he would find in that half attached diaper. So he finished strapping it on the body. He would put off changing the diaper as long as he could.

James picked out clothes to put on the nearly nude body. He was no fashion expert, but lucky for him the closet had limited offerings. Two pairs of stained pants that James had laundered nearly every day since Jeffrey had arrived. James grabbed the first pair he saw, blue slacks. A few flannel shirts that James had never seen Jeffrey wear were also hung up. James grabbed one along with a white T-shirt out of a dresser drawer as he worried the flannel alone would be too itchy. James knew he shouldn't be scared, all that lay on the bed was a bundle of atoms whose bonds were already breaking. Still, James tried not to step on cracks, was very careful with mirrors, and had never walked under a ladder. He approached Jeffrey's body with irrational fear and reverence that all bodies demand by their very existence.

James spoke to Jeffrey the same as he always did when providing care. "Jeffrey, I am going to change you now, I hope that's okay?" He waited for an answer; it didn't come. Gingerly, James touched the body. The flesh was stiff if not rigid. Rigor mortis is not a moment in time. It is a gradual change. Jeffrey's' body wasn't cold yet, but it wasn't warm either. Tepid maybe, like a baby's bathwater. Life left some residue in the flesh but only some. The instant of death does change a body, but all that death has in store for flesh takes time.

A dead body is a heavy and unhelpful thing. James was lucky in that Jeffrey's body wasn't wearing any clothes. Taking off clothing can be even more difficult than putting them on a dead person. Half the work was already done and James was glad for that. "Okay Jeffrey, I am going to put on your shirt now." As the kid spoke, he rolled the undershirt sleeve up in his hand and slipped it over Jeffrey's right arm. He had to pick Jeffrey's body up into a prone position and hold it up with one elbow hooked over the shoulder as he slipped the head into the neck hole. Jeffrey's chin pushed down against his chest; it appeared painful. James said, "I'm sorry," as he pushed Jeffrey's head up and through the neck hole. It would've hurt, but the man was dead. Still the kid felt bad.

It was a struggle getting the left arm in the arm hole. This time, James held up the body with his left hand. Twice he lost his grip and the body fell to the mattress with force. James apologized both times but kept at it. He was sweating by the time the undershirt was on. It kind of rode up in the back, which might have been uncomfortable, but again, Jeffrey was dead. James got the flannel. This was less of a problem as it was a button up shirt. Still, once James had wrestled both arms into the sleeves there was something strange and even intimate about buttoning a dead man's shirt. James looked Jeffrey in the face almost nose to nose as he did his work. Jeffrey's mouth was still open and a liquid, body fluid of some kind, dripped ever so slightly down his chin. Just as James had almost finished the roommate let out a huge snore causing the kid to jump, rocking the body in the bed.

"Okay Jeffrey, I am going to change your diaper now," James said as he undid one side of the product's tabs. He was expecting the worst but all he found was a little mucus-like smear in the diaper. The kid was relieved. Getting the pants on was an even sweatier and more miserable endeavor, but eventually Jeffrey was all dolled up and ready for his last big show. A sweating James sat back in Jeffrey's recliner, worn out. "Well Jeffrey, you're looking good." Jeffrey looked like a disheveled man permanently screaming at nothing.

James caught his breath and said a little prayer. Not something that came naturally to him but something he felt an urge to do. Later that night he would take a shot at his corner bar for Jeffrey and wish him well, whatever that meant. James picked himself up from the recliner and walked out of the room, looking back one last time at the now-dressed man lying on top of the bed. Within a few hours the rest of the family would arrive, say their goodbyes, and the body would be taken off to be cremated. The roommate was kind enough to remain silent for the family to pay their final respects. There would be no service.

Interlude

When We Become Sacramental

Western church historians have long speculated that the traditions of wrapping altars with rails and covering eucharistic elements with curtains or palls began in the first centuries of the church simply as a means of keeping goats and flies from wandering in and consuming them before the holy flock.

This may be the case. Nonetheless, I am suspicious. Speculations such as these must have taken shape in a room full of Protestants. Their hermeneutics, suspicious, stuck to the roofs of their mouths, painting their tongues, contriving a coat to prevent their buds from tasting—and thus their hearts from seeing—the full Godness present in and as the stuff.

This is the only scenario I can imagine.

A goat-prevention device! A shoo-er of flies!

Only to hearts with demystified eyes could these smirking speculations belong.

But perhaps that's beside the point. This error of arrogance (this degradation of the significance of sacred concealers) could be corrected quickly with a transient and not even thorough glance at the Hebrew Bible alone—not to mention other historical documents and sacred texts.

Accounts here will remind any student of history that acts such as containing, shielding, and even barricading holy stuff were common religious practices among ancient people. The Decalogue, preserved in the Ark of the Covenant, never saw the light of day. The ark itself lived in a tabernacle. Curtains drawn. Incense burning. Even its smells were obscured.

Radicalized by years of chasing the wind, Solomon tightened these restraints, building a padded cell. *More curtains!* he decreed. More pillars.

More smoke. More cherubim. So tightly were the curtains drawn, it has been reported by several prophets, that even in the form of a furious storm, the voice of God could not escape.

This room, Solomon called holy. The holiest. The Holy of Holies.

The practice of covering holy stuff is nothing new.

It is ancient and far predates the covering of eucharistic elements.

Underlying this practice, as you may have already expected, are both *theological* and (for lack of a universal term) *sacramental* convictions. We will touch on each of these below, beginning with the sacramental.

SACRAMENTAL

If we wish to begin to understand how the ancients perceived holy stuff, we need to say, from the outset, that the ancients *did not* regard this holy stuff to be God. Or gods. Or anything comparable. The holy stuff was no substitute for the divine. But, it wasn't regarded as *mere stuff* either. This is because the stuff, it was understood, had been, in one way or another, uniquely *touched*.

As Moses' face retained a holy glow long after his descent from the mountain, and as a dog leaves nose smudges on a window of a car that will last for decades—and more—so, upon this holy stuff, it was believed, something of God remained. Enough of God that, even when God was absent, something of God, there, in the room, was present.

Because of the holy stuff, the Holy was always at hand.

Anachronistically, this is the understanding to which we refer when we use the word *sacramental.*

THEOLOGICAL

Clearly, this understanding is brimming with beauty. So beautiful it is, that it ought to compel us to ask (as many have): *In light of this beautiful belief, why, rather than venerating them out in the open, putting them on parade or on display, did communities, instead, choose to hide such holy things away?* The answer to this question is found in yet another ancient understanding that we have simply called the theological.

For centuries before and after the church was founded (and in many places all over the world today) it was typically taught that the act of looking at God could only ever result in disaster. The Infinite Spirit was far too much for our frail, finite flesh. A glance toward the Great Expanse would be crushing. Upon direct exposure or any kind of eye contact, simply put, we would immediately explode.

Most people in those days wanted to avoid explosion. But they also desired to be near to God. And so it was in the tension between this repulsion and this urge that yet another question arose. Decade after decade and year after year, it would be asked: *How do you think we could do both?* The answer to *this* question was uncovered one day as a few people sat together in a sacred space pondering the holy stuff around them.

On this stuff lived God's fingerprints. This they believed. A piece of the Divine Creator. The sacred surplus of the Most High. And so on. Surely this stuff was not God. I guess . . . well, not exactly. But it wasn't *not* God, either. A love letter. A familiar perfume. Lint in a trap. Van Gogh's ear in the mail. Perhaps this wasn't God. Or not all of God. Nonetheless, something of God remained.

This brings us back to the space where the sacramental and theological meet. Astounding as this all was, the whole thing also triggered certain fears. *If looking at God can blow us up, and something of God is here, we better be careful with this stuff,* they reasoned. And so they were.

They covered it.

And, clothed though it was, simply sitting near to it, knowing it was once touched by the Beyond, transformed them. It was as if they had been born again, lying a-wiggle in the laughing lap of a kind Mother's love.

For these people,

Proximity was presence enough.

And no one exploded.

There was once a rabbi whose body was human. He made a troubling yet fascinating claim. He claimed that, at all times and in every moment, his very being was both touching and being touched by the presence of the divine.

Dirty hair, desert shoes, he had laid upon Her lap.

To wiggle in this way. To abide in God. For God and God's kindom to abide within. These were the rabbi's wishes. And his benediction. His hope for those he loved. One day at suppertime he showed them how this could be so.

What the ancients did not know, I reveal to you. Staring with the eyes will lead to explosion. This is well known. But I say to you: it is possible, also, for one to see with the tongue. Taste and see that the Lord is good! He invited them. And that evening, a sacrament was born.

In those early days, only two or three of them exploded.

Of course, this is something most people wished to avoid. But they also wanted to be near to God. *How do you think we could do both?* they asked. They returned to tradition in search of an answer. Old wine for new skins. And it was there that they found it.

Sometimes I envy those unenchanted Protestants. There must be great peace in a heart that cannot conceive of wrath or of demons or of judgments or of hells. But I imagine there's a lot of sadness, too. And heartbreak. I imagine their lives are lived like a funeral. A constant mourning and remembrance. Of the magical. Of the metaphysical. And of a god that once was.

Whatever the case, they were wrong. As they often are. The coverings atop the elements were not placed to keep them safe from goats and flies. Rather, they were placed so that no one would explode.

A protective measure utilized until the time of the tasting.

The Kindom of God is within you.

Gulp.

And so it was.

PS, JEFF:

Like the other stuff, death is holy, too.

In our last days, our bodies sense that it's close. Jeff's body knew it. Ours will know it, too. And the chaplains will be sent a-knocking. Slightly crazed but well-meaning eyes, they will dig in an old wooden box. *Take and eat*, they will vow. *This is the Body of God.*

Politely (quietly) we will laugh. We will know that, even if we could swallow, there would be no need. The thief in the night has already broken in. Smashing the cabinets. Squeezing elastic walls.

He's here. But really he's already gone. So they'll begin to burn incense. And pop popcorn. And with white sheets and white towels and white walls washed yellow beneath fluorescent lights, they will cover us.

Waiting. To place pennies on our eyes.

Waiting. To toss a rose.

They will cover and they'll wait.

Not for closure.

But for fear.

That too much exposure might make them explode.

17

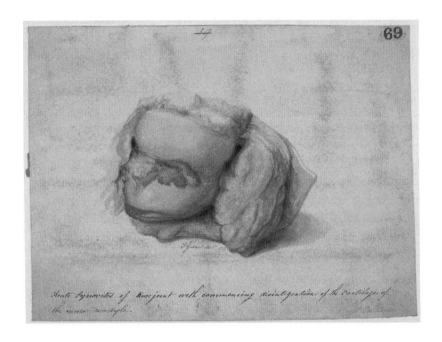

Acute Synovitis of knee joint with commencing disintegration of the Cartilage of the inner condyle.

CHAPTER TWO

Kim's Bed Sore

Imagine a room. It's well appointed, overly appointed. There are satin sheets, 10,000-thread-count Egyptian cotton comforters. Decorative pillows that are good for nothing lay strewn about the place. The room smells strongly of perfume, too strongly of perfume. There are other smells in the room as well. They mingle with that perfume and create a kind of amalgamated stink, gathered from too many sources.

The room is filled with signs of an extraordinary life. Pictures cover every free space. Every ledge on the desk in the corner, hung on the walls, lining the windowsills. Pictures of exotic vacations, exclusive visits to famous places. There are pictures of the now bedridden woman at the pyramids sitting astride a bored-looking camel. There are pictures from the deck of a beautiful yacht floating in the Mediterranean Sea. There are pictures with political figures and entertainment stars. These pictures are meant to present to those entering the room a portrait of an extraordinary life. They are to let those who enter know they are among greatness.

The room sits in the back of a huge penthouse. Kim had moved there when the stairs of her town brownstone got to be too much. The penthouse had a grand dining room, a jacuzzi tub, a movie theater, a chef's kitchen with professional appliances and a massive Sub-Zero fridge. The place was designed to host lavish parties, to be a lavish penthouse where one could see and be seen.

A veranda wrapped its way around the entire penthouse offering "unparalleled views" of the city. It has been three years since Kim had sunned herself on that balcony. The fridge hasn't held real food in ages, outside of the lunch meat, microwavable dinners, and bags of take-out the caregiver kept inside—its only other contents being bottled water, feeding tube solution, feeding tubes, and an old jar of mayo that had been in there since Kim moved in. Hopefully they would never get confused. The jacuzzi hasn't been used in years, Kim's spa days now involved wet wipes and new sheets. Kim no longer got out of bed for a bath, or dinner, or anything else. The movie theater got regular use though. In there Kim's caregiver used the big screen to Zoom with her relatives, both across town and back in Poland. Seeing them on the big screen is as close as she can get to being with them in real life.

The past few years of Kim's life had not been extraordinary. They had been normal. Kim got older and her body got sick. The people she depended on had gotten older themselves, many had died, few could be of any help. Kim had kids; the kids loved Kim, but they had their own lives and responsibilities. The people in the pictures on the wall were largely dead and buried. That or they had drifted away years prior. Much of the world had simply drifted away from Kim.

There Kim lay, alone and bored. Sitting doesn't mean stagnation. Kim, like all living things, continued to change. She lost muscle tone, her flesh sagging and thinning. For years she had kept aging at bay. There were medical professionals, various injections. There were dietary supplements and exercise routines, but time comes for us all. Eventually the risk of infection became too great and so the shots and injections stopped. Eventually the body couldn't lift the weights or climb the stairs. Kim couldn't take in the nutrition she needed to sustain herself. So it goes, all attempts to stop aging add up to spitting in the wind.

Eventually it got to where Kim could no longer hold herself up on the toilet. Another perfectly ordinary event, which happens to most people who live long lives, and an event society does its best to ignore. For years Kim had worn, or perhaps been wrapped in, adult diapers. At first, when Kim could still get to the bathroom, Kim wore "pull-ups" or "briefs" as they were called. There was a picture on the pull-ups bag of a young woman playing tennis. It was supposed to make the person buying the pull-ups think that their loved one could still be active. The lady playing tennis was not wearing nor did she need to wear pull-ups.

The pull-ups lasted a while though they normally were never "pulled" down, but instead were torn at the seams and removed when soiled. They gave Kim a measure of dignity or at least that is what their package led one to believe. Eventually, once Kim was stuck in bed, the pull-ups could no longer contain the urine and stool. The caregivers switched to regular diapers.

The regular diapers were larger and bulkier. They bunched up in places but they were more absorbent. The caregiver could leave them on longer without the waste leaking out the sides and on to the bed. This meant less sheets to wash. At night the caregiver would put two of these diapers on Kim. That way when the changing took place in the middle of the night, she only had one to be removed and the sheets were relatively safe from spillage. It was a common practice that the caregiver and millions of other caregivers before had used on scores of patients. It was an ordinary procedure, but not one without costs.

What follows is the story of the bed sore that broke open on Kim's coccyx area. The bed sore began its life as most bed sores do. Kim was unable to take in enough nutrients or to process enough nutrients to be able to properly perfuse and gather enough energy to get out of bed. The issues around nutrition didn't stop there. Kim developed what is called protein calorie malnutrition. An extremely common ailment near the end of life, it basically meant that Kim was not taking in enough or making use of enough nutrients to survive. As a result her tissues, muscle, and fat below the skin thinned out and became weak. At the same time the constant pressure of laying in bed caused a small red spot to form on the coccyx.

Now this was not the only sore on Kim's body. There are others; put a feeding tube in a bedridden person and they will get sores. People become Swiss cheese if they linger too long. The sore on Kim's coccyx is simply the wound of interest for this particular story. This red spot, it didn't hurt, it wasn't painful. If you pushed on it the spot would turn white, like pushing on a sunburn, and could stay that way for hours. This was because the blood was not returning to the area.

This sore may have been avoidable by turning and moving Kim more often. Keeping Kim clean and dry and in different positions could possibly, not in all cases, but possibly have made a difference. Only that didn't happen. Kim's caregiver, and the person who filled in for that caregiver when she was allowed to leave on the weekend, were fine caregivers. Kim's primary caregiver was always nice and polite, thoughtful about the care she gave. But she worked five days in a row, twenty-four hours a day, and things eventually can begin to slip away. Kim was not the caregiver's mother. Not only that but Kim wasn't light, and sometimes it was hard for the caregiver to move her. If she were to hurt herself, to pull a muscle or pinch a nerve in her back, who would take care of Kim? As such, Kim sat still longer than she should have. This along with the protein calorie malnutrition caused the red dot. The small unopened but discolored piece of flesh began to rip apart. When that happened Kim's bed sore was truly born into the world.

Bed sores, including Kim's, develop in stages. They grow in a predictable way and humans have come up with classifications for various stages in that growth. The classification goes from stage one to stage four and then beyond stage four something called unstageable. Each stage is worse than the one before. Kim's bed sore, when it was just a little spot, was a stage-one bed sore. Things got worse from there.

Taking care of a person in Kim's condition is not a hard task, it's an impossible task. It's not unlike caring for a newborn baby. Only newborn babies won't cause serious back pain when you attempt to roll them around. Newborn babies won't say offensive and rude things to their caregivers. Newborn babies are fresh and new, they are growing fat and muscle and weight, not shedding it. Newborn babies rarely develop the C-diff infection causing endless watery stool that burns through flesh like battery acid. More than that newborn babies are largely cared for by their parents who are willing to take the sleepless nights and endless days simply because they love their child. Kim's caregiver didn't mind Kim, she knew Kim was her source of income, but it would be hard to say she loved Kim.

As such, sometimes Kim didn't get changed. Sometimes Kim was left to soak in her own waste. Human waste when combined with protein calorie malnutrition, lack of oxygen due to pressure, and time caused that little red "stage one" bed sore to grow. First it split open. The flesh, which was still alive, just kind of ripped apart. It did this under the surface of the wound, occluded from the outside world. It hurt, it hurt horribly, as the nerves were all still intact. The pain of flesh slowly separating, ripping, and tearing was unbearable, but Kim had long since lost the ability to make her pain known. The only sound the caregiver heard was a slight moan, and the only sign she saw of the pain was the wince on Kim's face whenever she was moved. This added to the caregiver simply letting Kim lay in place. She didn't want to move Kim and cause more pain.

It should have stopped before it reached stage two, perhaps if Kim was better cared for, not by an employee but by someone who loved her like their own newborn baby, it would have been stopped. There were creams and treatments, honey dressing and bandages that could have been placed on the wound. The wound was rarely properly cleaned and dressed. Sometimes new dressings were just placed over the old ones so that the wound looked cared for when really it wasn't. But it was only a red spot, at least that's what the caregiver thought. She was unaware of what was going on under the flesh, deep in the tissue.

Then one day it came to a head. The small red mark not only burst apart but a large pus filled blister formed at the top of Kim's behind. The flesh around it was bright red and hot to the touch. It hurt badly, the wound was growing, but nothing changed in the care. A wound nurse was called out to the apartment. This nurse cleaned and bandaged the wound, medicated it and put on a protective barrier cream. When the nurse left the wound appeared to be managed, but it would require a complicated maintenance routine and that never materialized.

The bandages were not changed regularly. Kim was not repositioned as often as prescribed. The diaper was left wet for far too long. This may seem like negligence but it isn't or if it is then nearly all people totally dependent on paid caregivers are being neglected. It would have been worse at the nursing home.

That said, even if Kim had been well cared for, if the proper creams had been applied, if Kim had been moved, propped up, and repositioned, it is hard to know what would have become of the bed sore. Not enough nutrition was being taken in. What was dumped down the feeding tube the body had little ability to process. The feedings pooled in her belly and in her chest, making Kim weaker and weaker and more and more uncomfortable. Eventually food isn't food, it's poison.

Without proper nutrition, healing the wound was next to impossible and so the bed sore continued to do what bed sores do. It grew and dived itself deeper into Kim's body. The technical term for this is "tunneling." Eventually the blister that had formed over the sore burst and the pus was absorbed by the open flesh. This was a bad thing as the pus was full of bacteria that infected the skin around the wound. Neither Kim nor the caregiver would ever know when this happened. Sometime in the middle of the night. It was hard to notice any changes with all the pain Kim was feeling; hurt just kind of bled into hurt. The next morning, the moment the caregiver decided it was time to actually change the bandage, everyone and everything in a forty foot radius would smell the change.

The caregiver pulled the bandage off, which hurt furiously as it pulled on the red worn skin all around the wound. Some of that skin came off, ripping the wound wider. The bandage was soaked. The flesh around the now gaping wound had turned black. It was open roughly the size of a palm. A window inside the hidden world of Kim's lower spine. The wound had "tunneled" past her skin and deep into the fatty layers and muscle beneath. When the caregiver first smelled the necrotic inky black flesh she let out a slight yelp. She couldn't help it, the stink hit her like a punch in the face, the visual of the open body turned her stomach. She had to leave the room or risk retching in front of Kim. The caregiver had seen bed sores before, even stage three sores but there is no getting used to looking through a hole in a person where no hole should be, and smelling dead flesh cannibalizing its own living tissue. After seeing and smelling the wound, the caregiver refused to care for it any longer. All wound care was left to the wound nurse who came only once a week.

Kim's bed sore continued to grow, spread, and tunnel. The infection became worse, reaching its poisonous fingers into Kim's blood. Fevers and chills assailed her. The pain increased, as did the pus and drainage. One day while the wound care nurse was changing the dressings, Kim's sister Courtney had stopped by for a visit. Courtney wanted to be in the room when the dressing was removed. She wanted to know what her sister was dealing with.

By this point the wound had progressed past stage three and on to four. The wound care nurse was pleased that Courtney was there to see the wound care. It's good for a family to know what is really happening to their loved one's body, but it's rare they actually see it. The wound care nurse removed the outer bandage and immediately the stink filled the room. The room was thick with the stench of death, of decay, of waste, and poison. The human body is designed to recoil from such scents, to go the other way. It was hard but Courtney steeled herself. The nurse then removed the old packing.

Kim's bed sore was now a giant void in her body and that void needed to be filled. The nurse when changing the old dressing used cotton to "pack" the open space. It was time to change out and replace that old soiled packing. Carefully the nurse began to remove the strips of cotton that had been inserted into Kim's bed sore. Courtney imagined one or two strips of cotton, just enough to fill a small cut. But the nurse kept removing strip after strip. More and more unnatural material was pulled from Kim's bed sore until a mound of the old packing sat on a cloth the nurse had spread near the head of the bed. It was a mercy that Kim's face was looking away, not that anyone knew how much her eyes saw anymore. A mountain of material, piled half a foot high, of wet black cotton sat at the top of the bed. A mountain of illness and death. Courtney didn't want to look but her eyes happened to catch a glimpse into the roundish jagged wound. Now a full five inches in diameter. Courtney saw her sister's tailbone. She saw it clear as day, looking like part of a Thanksgiving day turkey carcass. Tendons hanging off of it, pus and biological film somewhat obscuring it, but there was no denying that this was her sister's skeleton. It seemed impossible. Courtney's mind searched for another, any other, explanation for what she was seeing, but there wasn't any.

Humans are mostly hidden, we are like the earth in that way. The parts that are seen are just the crust, what holds it up remains occulted by our flesh. We don't even know it but we find comfort in this. Looking into another person is like looking into an active volcano. Seeing what exists beneath the known. The gelatinous substances that pulsate and ooze through the body. Looking into a person is a horror and it comes with a cost. Courtney swallowed hard trying not to vomit. There was no way to swallow back the tears that dripped. Then the wound care nurse set to the task of debriding Kim's bedsore.

The wound had become a home to invasive bacteria. The bacteria fed off the dead cells. The dead parts of Kim gave life to bacteria which then, like all life, wanted more and more, wanted to spread and grow and breed, and so the nurse debrides. To debride a wound is to remove the dead, to take away the slough of decay, and starve out the bacteria. The nurse set out her instruments on a sterile paper pad that lay on the bed next to Kim. She laid out her tools methodically. Each one wrapped up in a single-use bag, safe and sterile—scissors and gauze, packets of solutions. The nurse opened it all up and then knelt down to look into the wound.

Watching the nurse work was like watching a toddler feed itself. The nurse's hands disappeared into the hole. Swabs wiped around its interior. Chemicals were applied, tissues removed. It was a sloppy, painful thing to watch. The flesh on the sides of the wound, already red and agitated, pushed up and spread apart by the probing hands of the healer. Kim let out a moan or two, the only sound she ever made anymore. She recoiled, her weak and contracted legs tried, pathetically, to kick and move away from the gloved hands. The nurse grabbed Kim's hip tightly to hold her in place. Sweat dripped from the straining nurse's brow.

It was at this moment—watching her sister struggle, watching the nurse strain to keep her in place, smelling the chemicals mixed with death and waste—that sick warmth rushed over Courtney, like a fever shaking her to her core. All she could do was step out of the room and onto the balcony. It was the first time someone had stepped out onto the balcony in years. Courtney sucked in fresh air and tried to forget what she had just seen. Later she would tell the family an approximation of the day's events. She couldn't bring herself to truly describe it; to do so would have meant to hold the horror before her face again and that would be too much.

As such the story didn't truly describe Kim's wound. Courtney didn't discuss the filmy yellow pus that spread across the bottom quarter of the hole, broken in places but holding fast. The story didn't go into the stench of death, which caused Courtney to throw out her clothes when she got home. She didn't touch on the depth of the wound, the color of the bone, or the shape of the tendons. Courtney couldn't bring herself to mention the struggle between what was left of Kim and the nurse trying to hold her in place. Because the family didn't get the whole story they didn't truly grasp the suffering. Sure they were concerned, there was no lack of love, but even if Courtney had described the scene perfectly, what would they do about it? How much more care could money buy? They had lives and work. They couldn't do the caregiving, and even if they could they wouldn't know where to start.

The sore continued to grow. Deeper and deeper, if one wanted to they could have stuck their arm into Kim's bed sore and reached all the way up to the back of her neck. By this point the wound had become unstageable, no bottom to be found. It would never heal. The infection would kill Kim, not officially. Officially it would be the dementia that treated her so cruelly and took so much from her. The wound took as well; it took too much—so much that its host would succumb. The end of Kim would be in the sweat and gore of active infection, but it would be an end to pain and fear. The end of Kim would not be extraordinary, in fact it would be incredibly and utterly ordinary. It happens every single day, and that is the true horror of it all.

Interlude

The Un-cooking

THE HIGH TABLE

The children of the Turning appeared among us and the promise of heaven's fire was stolen from the skies. Here below, it was converted into the fires of the heart: passion for poets, hope for the poor, and rising tides of tension carrying deliberate demands to be doled out to the powers of the earth.

Before those days, this table sat right here. And since its placement it had never been moved. It was magical then. And the mere thought of displacing an object of magical import would have seemed abhorrent and untoward.

The people who built it called the table *High*. And so they placed it. A few steps upward, yet reachable. Catching and yet stretching the eye from its surface, up through the ceiling, and into the stars.

Here it stayed. Safe. Secured. Anchored to the wall. Fixed firmly to the floor. Until the Time of the Turning.

THE LOWER FEAST

Those who knew hunger's agony in those days were countless—so that societies of love-doers swelled. Though, families at their side, members of these groups would frequent the table called *High*, more often than not, one would find the love-doers dwelling in the spaces just below. In basements and cellars, and in halls named for saints, they mixed secrets with wishes and heat, transmuting roots and animals' flesh.

As they washed that last utensil and wiggled the final table into place, a line would form, eroded and exhausted, just outside the house built for gods. Simmering scents ascending as incense. Stews to fill the stomachs of the faint.

THE HIGH FEAST

So also, up the steps, past the cob-webbed corners and tattered collections of once used books, at this table called *High*, the community priest would make ready a meal of his own. Coffee-stained vestments gilded, whispered words, and magic in his hands, however, no savory perfume graced the air as the result of his work. On the contrary. Here, the already-prepared was transmuted in reverse. The cooked was made raw—changed anew into the salty, warm-bloody flesh of their gods.

Bowing in reverence as they approached, some would not rise until they had kissed the floor. *Taste and see!* they would greet one another before their meal, un-cooked, was consumed.

UNKNOWNS

Beyond these limited details regarding the rites performed and the people who gathered around this table called *High*, our knowledge, at best, is incomplete. Artifacts, manuscripts, and other clues surface occasionally. These spark conversations and promise new insights. At the end of the day, however, more often than not, seekers and scholars alike have been left with a bit more mystery than any kind of real clarity.

That's not to say that these conversations are fruitless. On the contrary. Any student of the table is immediately exposed to a treasure trove of ancient knowledges, complex spiritualities, perspectives, and practices that, had that student not engaged in the subject, would have been impossible to imagine or comprehend.

No doubt, this kind of exposure is a gift. For this reason, I'm incredibly grateful to have some time with you today to re-enter into dialogue with the scholars whose attention and imagination, much like my own, has been captivated and sparked around the table.

In our time together, we will be visiting four prominent hypotheses regarding the table: the apotheotic, the cardial, the intermundia, and the contradecubitus. Though their names may sound unfamiliar, I assure you that their content is well worth our journey, and I'm confident you'll enjoy what we find along the way.

Thanks for being here. Let's begin.

The Apotheotic Hypothesis

Circulated especially among the universities nearest to the Great Sea, our first hypothesis of interest posits that the ritual act of un-cooking, presided over by a priest, was appropriated and adapted from the practices of magicians who, today, we might describe as "even more ancient," than those who utilized the table here.

In fables and fairy tales, these *more ancients* spoke of those who were born *heroes*, creatures (much like us) who dwelt among us in the early generations of the earth. These were not the kind of heroes we celebrate today with banners and parades and politicians' speeches—those perceived by the public as vocationally sacrificing (or vocationally giving away) their own individual lives for the sake of an Other or for the sake of a Whole.

Rather, in these communities, a hero was one regarded as half-human and half-god. On better days, you could find heroes subduing monsters, slaying dragons, and stoning giants—providing valiant defenses against any whose mission it was to terrorize the villagers, the vulnerable, or the poor. On other days, the behavior of a hero could be embarrassing.

The apotheotic hypothesis submits that in table communities, everyday people, distressed by one bully or another, would gather to consume the flesh of their gods in hopes of becoming *heroic* (meaning *hero-like*) themselves: human, and yet growing a bit more into something of a god.

After eating, devotees would describe a sense of burning in their chests accompanied by a brief dizziness followed by a feeling of being *wrapped in a blanket of eternity*, a phenomenon that became commonly known as the Great Shedding. In this spiritual state, community members believed, pieces of their humanity were breaking away, making room for an influx of the divine. Now *heroized*, the faithful would be given a hero's charge: to fight fights, to vanquish the demonic, and to defend the poor, the widow, the orphan, and all who were dispossessed.

As is true of most hypotheses, the apotheotic has not been received without controversy. Parchment fragments from unearthed sixth-century collections of mythical tales and religious rites, however, do suggest that in several table communities (and particularly in those around the Great Sea) this understanding was prominent—both in the practices of long-time community members as well as in the testimonies of their proselytes.

The Cardial Hypothesis

Our second hypothesis of interest is known as the cardial. Conversations regarding the cardial hypothesis have recently emerged in a number of disparate circles. Not unlike those who claim allegiance to the apotheotic, cardial subscribers hold that the traditions of the table were borrowed. Yet, unlike the heroizers of the apotheotic camp, cardial scholars posit that the traditions of the table were likely inherited from those ancients whose gods were known to dwell somewhere within (or beyond) the basins and bottles of the night.

Like most sects, the convictions of these communities were often paradoxical. Whether the goal was to be drunk, to dissipate, to float outward beyond bodily bounds, *on the one hand,* or to dive deeply into one's self without the distraction of the body's uninebriated senses, *on the other,* the strong belief of these "more ancient sects" was that red rosacea and rolling eyes were means toward a mode of being in which one could taste and feel the overwhelming presence of otherwise imperceptible gods.

As table communities began to appropriate and incorporate these beliefs into their own, they paid particular attention to the pious veneration that these elationist and dipsophiliac communities (as they were known) directed toward the chalice itself. This devotion was best exemplified in the rich materials with which the chalice was crafted, and in the rare stones that bedazzled it so that, when elevated, it sparkled. Table communities adopted this tradition. To this day, you can find their chalices in museums and in the houses built for gods (like this one), which have now become museums themselves. Incidentally, cults devoted exclusively to the chalice have been a recurring phenomenon throughout the centuries—both within and outside the borders of table communities.

One of the most prominent departures from (or modifications to) the dipsophiliac inheritance occurred when, in the third century, the communities convened an ingathering at which they affirmed that it was *not* necessary to have intoxicating amounts of libations (or intoxicants at all) in the cup in order to receive the cup's benefits. To the *more ancients*, of course, this move would have been baffling if not scandalous. But by the third century, what was once a borrowed ritual was now a solemn rite with liturgical, gesticual, thaumaturgical, and theological meanings of its own.

In addition to adopting the decorated cup and yet unmandating the alcohol that it was once created to hold, the table communities also distinguished themselves from the dipsophiliacs in their convictions about the direction and the goal of the divine, as well as the manner in which the divine was believed to "take place" in their ceremonies around the table.

While the spiritual longings of the dipsophiliacs were aimed (by way of the cup and its contents) toward an experience of the gods through an intoxicated or orgasmic displacement or *moving out* of one's self. The table communities, in contrast, had come to desire their gods *to move in*.

In a similar vein, table communities took the dipsophiliac desensitization and traded it for tangibility. They wished to taste and touch their gods with senses intact. And for them, the table was the setting in which that desire was fulfilled.

Here, gods were summoned and consumed. The chalice as their vehicle, the mouth of the believer was their entry-point. Once inside, gods would find their way to the heart. And it was there, according to the first languages of the sect, that they would raise their tent, hang their hammock, or build their holy abode.

These shifts in understanding had clear impacts on the newly faithful. Believing their bodies were god-houses, they would adorn themselves with sacred tattoos, elaborate piercings, bright paraments, and other suitable works of art. Many would exercise daily, abstaining from various foods, and being careful to eat only that which would be pleasing to divine tongues.

Holding that the number of gods a heart could house was limitless, even already-inhabited members of these communities would continue to gather weekly with the rest, praying at the table that more and more gods might find their bodies to be suitable quarters for living.

The Intermundia Hypothesis

Widening the scope of inquiry beyond the possibility of *more ancient* influences on table communities alone, our third hypothesis, embraced primarily in the north, pays close attention to the location and positioning of the tables themselves in relation to their physical surroundings.

As you may have noticed as you arrived this morning, beyond the parking lot, countless monuments remain standing outside of this *house* to this day, embedded there proudly in the sand. This is not an uncommon sight. For millennia, table communities would bury the bodies of their dead just beyond the eastern wall of the house.

It is thought that this practice performed two symbolic functions. First, it kept loved ones near; and second, as a nod toward the morning sun, it also came to represent, for many, the hope of a mystical new day when death would be defeated as an enemy and sorrow would be cast into a pit.

As you might imagine, something of an emotional cycle ensued in the faithful as a result of these functions and this placement. Buried close, the memory of the dead would evoke grief, opening old wounds as, on the way in, one walked by the body of someone they loved. These wounds, now opened, would be dressed by an ornery and unrelenting hope—a spiritual hope for a coming new day about which this community proclaimed. And so they would be healed, so to speak, until the next passing by, the next reopening of the wounds, the next subsequent healing by hope, and so on. This dynamic was complicated by that which took place inside of the building—specifically at and around this table called *High*—for here, more than memory, pain, and healing were taking place in, with, and through the practitioners.

Scholars who champion the intermundia hypothesis observe that, for centuries, the tables inside of houses built for gods were built directly into the eastern walls, extending outward from the stonework. Others were simply placed or fastened there.

The placement of the table in this way performed two functions. First, it ensured that when community members faced the table, they would also be facing the eastern wall. Second, it ensured that, in looking at the wall, they would also be looking *through* the wall, gazing at and remembering those who were memorialized on the other side.

These placements—of the table inside and of the monuments outside—were no mistake. For, according to the intermundial hypothesis, this community believed that much like a table in everyday life, in a kitchen or in a dining room, the table called *High* was a *meeting place*. A place of reunion. An adjoining of two distinct worlds and of the residents who inhabited them.

Here, at the table, a drink was poured. Heads were bowed. And melodies were murmured softly. This would go on for a while until the sounds, bouncing wall to wall to wall to wall, would give way to something more. Those singing would gradually begin to perceive sounds that they themselves were not creating.

Ancient texts reveal that participants believed that these voices—beyond their own—were generated by two distinct communities. First, they claimed, these were the voices of invisible choirs of magical creatures. Glowing and flapping, these creatures hovered, covering feet, in the presence of a great fire that burned brightly upon a gilded throne. Second, it was believed that, somehow, in the charming of the table, in the presence of the flapping, and at the simple ringing of what archaeologists now refer to as *the dinner bell*, the loved ones of those gathered, buried beyond the eastern wall, for a moment, would be quickened and awake.

Vivified and filled with feelings of unification, these buried beloveds would enter into the songs being sung. Aunties and uncles, children and siblings, parents, fathers, and moms could all be heard—and in their own voices, the voices that were theirs when they were alive. They still got the words wrong. And they still sang off-key. All of that. But those little things that used to be annoying to their families didn't seem to matter so much anymore. They were here. And present. And un-alchemized. For a moment, they were transmuted backward. Flesh once rotting, recomposed. Audible. And somehow tangible. Pressed in tightly, close. Skin upon skin upon heart.

Desert scrolls dating back to the third century contain a liturgical recitation meant to be delivered from the *table conjoined to the East*. The recitation includes instruction for both the conjuring of choirs and of a *communion of ancestors*. In the margin of the page, there is a hand-written note about encouraging those who gathered to sing *like they mean it*. For obvious reasons, the intermundia school claims these scrolls as evidence in support of their hypothesis.

The Contradecubitus Hypothesis

The fourth and final hypothesis of import to us, without which our survey would be incomplete, is known as the contradecubitus. Conversations regarding this hypothesis were sparked worldwide two decades ago after a routine dig in which three mosaics—all located within a one-mile radius—were unearthed by a renowned professor and a small group of university students.

In ruins of ancient houses built for gods, these mosaics laid undamaged beneath six feet of sand for millennia. Perhaps most striking—and most relevant for our conversation today—is each one's unique depiction of theological and thaumaturgical mythologies which, before two decades ago, had been lost to history and iterated allusively only in a small number of obscure and historically questionable documents.

At the very center of each mosaic, bright tiles are arranged to portray the scene of a meal. On the table sit two fish on a large blue plate. The plate is encircled by triangular pieces of bread. The people at the table are pressed into each other—with very little room for elbows or for movement alike. The abundance and closeness exhibited are perhaps intended to indicate the kind of celebratory feast that takes place in times of transition (i.e., a graduation party or a funeral luncheon today).

To the left of the meal scene a human figure is depicted. Its body is thin and androgynous, donning nothing but sackcloth. Save for two birds perched in a patch of shrubbery, this figure is alone, producing an auburn tear beneath a harvest moon.

To the right of the meal scene, a body similar in stature and build is found in isolation, as well. This body is stretched out upon a raised bed of stone made from the same *blue* as the plate at the feast. The body wears a nearly lifeless face, without expression, communicating to its observers that the end is nigh. Here, the single tear has been replaced by a number of larger auburn impressions. Striking in size, they clearly bear witness to a story of prolonged suffering, neglect, or abuse. Their placements suggest that they are the type of wound that forms on dying bodies once they have been abandoned in stone quarries or landfills.

As you know, abandonment in this style was not unpopular for families at the time the mosaics were produced. It was a culturally accepted option that offered the family certain benefits. First, the act of leaving the body alive produced in family members a sense of relief from the guilt that might otherwise be accrued in an ordinary (more instantaneous) act of matri- or patricide; while placing the body far off offered a special kind of *forgetfulness*—an interfamilial amnesia. That is, out of sight and out of mind, the body lost its special ability to burden and manipulate. Any sense of duty or obligation one might have felt to spend time tending to a degrading object that would never reciprocate one's love was squashed out, a flame beneath a bushel. Suffocated. Smoke. Abandonment in this style also offered closure in a way not often provided by the pageantry of a funeral.

Beyond the dissonant juxtaposition of the merry feast and the scenes of lonely suffering, perhaps the most striking image in the mosaic is the one situated atop all three. Here we find a body. Still androgynous. Still thin. But it has undergone a metamorphosis. The auburn impressions have purpled. The body's frame has taken a new posture. And a glow. Upright, proud, it hovers above the feasters who abandoned it. Some bow down. Some lift hands in postures of praise.

Subscribers to the contradecubitus hypothesis posit that before the assimilation of table communities into mainstream religiosity, the table was a space of celebration predominately curated and maintained by slab-sleepers and those who bled beneath moons. Though scars remained on these people—and on their gods—they nonetheless found themselves to be healed, loved, and strong. Purple, the color of scabbing, became for them a sign of royalty. And of the divine. And so they were: royals, gods, feasting sumptuously together, lacerations, boils, bruises, and scars, as they lived out the rest of their days together.

AS YOU LEAVE

Based on experience though it may be, it has been said that memory itself is an act of imagination. Every image recalled is an image generated anew. Though the hypotheses we've explored today are unproven and incomplete, the scenarios their scholars present as they sift through ancient sands in search of knowledges, meanings, and magics once infused into tables, trans-mutations, and gods, are invaluable. Though academic and occasionally dry, these are nonetheless stirring expositions fueled by curiosity, wonder, and desire. As such, they offer us glimpses not only into the enchantment of former times, but also into the wonders of what might yet be.

The heroizing desires of the apotheotic hypothesis, communities longing to live lives with meaning that rescue, slay, and save; the domiciling desires of the cardial hypothesis that hope to make the body a home, and to feel at home with death, with gods, and with the world; the unifying desires for communion with the dead of the intermundia hypothesis; and the desires to belong, to be valued, and to be held for one's whole life—and even in one's old age—of the contradecubitus hypothesis; though these desires are all ancient, they are also quite relevant, if not familiar to all of us, today.

Though this sacred place, to us, is a museum complete with gift shop and cafe, I hope that, perhaps, you will find a way to take with you something more than a magnet or an overpriced T-shirt as you go. I hope that, dipping your toes into the longings of the past, something in you was quickened or stirred. Perhaps your table will never be called *High*. But I do hope you give it a name.

RE-TURNING

The children of the Turning appeared among us and the promise of heaven's fire was stolen from the skies. Here below, it was converted into the fires of the heart: passion for poets, hope for the poor, and rising tides of tension carrying deliberate demands to be doled out to the powers of the earth.

Before those days, this table sat *here*.

It was full of magic.

Since the Turning, it has been dislocated.

Nonetheless, sometimes I like to sneak up here at night. I kiss the floor. I trace the holes with my hands where the anchors used to be. And I like to imagine that there's still something in them—some connection—to the gods, or to the beyond. I like to imagine that some of that fire was left behind. Something extra. For when our bodies fail. For when hope is no longer possible. For the time when we approach our own transmutation *backward* from warm salty flesh into food for the earth.

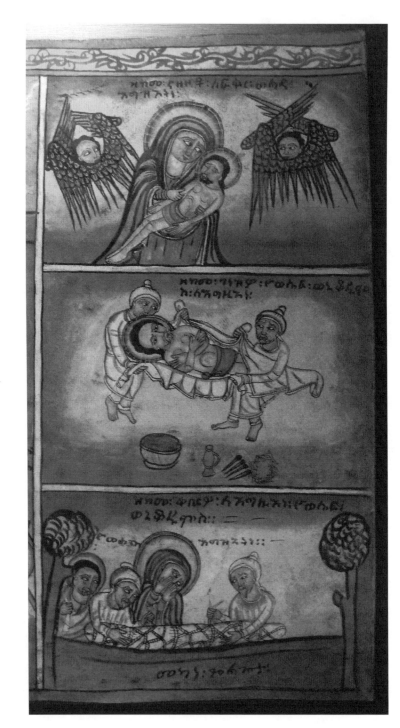

CHAPTER THREE

Elizabeth's Mommy

Elizabeth was sick for a while; nobody knew, but who was to know anyway? Elizabeth's family was mostly all dead. While she was only in her early seventies, the generation before her had all passed, and neither her mother nor her beloved aunt had any children, save Elizabeth herself. Elizabeth did not marry or have kids. She had money—a lot actually. Elizabeth lived in the same house she grew up in. It had been bought and paid for decades before she inherited the ranch. It wasn't much, three bedrooms, a bath and a half. Small, squat, and brick. The kind of place that could brush off an atomic bomb, the inhabitants protected by asbestos tiles and lead paint.

You could say it needed updates but "need" would be the wrong word. Elizabeth's dad, a product of the depression, had taken meticulous care of everything and taught Elizabeth to do the same. Nobody had ever actually stepped on the shag carpeting since it was put in. Clear plastic runners made sure that a guest could enjoy the aesthetic without setting foot on the brownish-tan material. The carpeting still looked clean and fluffy as the day her dad had put it in. Nothing had to be updated, the appliances worked as they had sixty years earlier when they were first installed; that doesn't mean things shouldn't have been updated.

The two couches were mostly wood cut into elaborate patterns, flowers and hearts, that gave a Victorian flair to the ancient furniture. To make these works of art actual couches, uncomfortable, upholstered cushions were inlaid into the wood at various places. Those cushions were then covered in plastic by Elizabeth's dad. Plastic that made crushing and farting sounds when a person moved on it. Nobody really sat in the sitting room. There wasn't even a TV in there. Elizabeth spent most of her time in her bedroom, as her parents had spent most of their time in theirs when they were alive.

Elizabeth's room was tiny. Located directly opposite the front door. A pinkish white paint colored the walls. Elizabeth's old man thought it was a nice color for a little girl when he painted the room for Elizabeth's tenth birthday. Maybe it was a little pinker at first and it had faded, maybe not. The carpet in Elizabeth's room was flat and worn, discolored and stained. It was lived-in carpet and probably the only thing in the home that truly needed replacement along with the carpet in Elizabeth's folks' room. The master bedroom was a mirror image of Elizabeth's room just down the hall. The rooms were separated by a bathroom. The bathroom worked fine though it had some wear. Spills, accidents, and wheelchair tires had done their damage.

Elizabeth spent her life in her room. She watched TV and read books about dogs. She loved dogs. After her mother died, which was after her father had died, Elizabeth took care of the family poodle for a while, but the dog had gone the way of Elizabeth's parents a few years earlier. While the dog was alive the dog's vet, the letter carrier, and a few of her mom's old church friends were about the only people Elizabeth still had any contact with. Once the dog died the list shrunk by a third.

It was the letter carrier who finally noticed something was wrong. Elizabeth always got her mail, always picked it up within minutes of it being dropped off. When it sat in the box unopened for a few days he knew something was up. He was worried Elizabeth might accuse him of being a peeping Tom (and she certainly would have) if she caught him looking through her window, but the letter carrier couldn't live with himself if he didn't try and figure out what was going on. One look into Elizabeth's room and his suspicions were confirmed. There was Elizabeth half on the bed and half off. Her mouth open, her face all screwed up and covered in spit and snot. The letter carrier called 911, though he was reasonably sure Elizabeth was dead already. Wouldn't be the first corpse he had run into in his career carrying letters.

The medics had to force the door open, which was not an easy task as Elizabeth had put a number of dead bolts on the old wooden door.

Eventually they were able to breach the threshold. They found Elizabeth covered in her own filth. She had a fever and was severely dehydrated. If she had been left for another day or two Elizabeth would not have made it. When they asked Elizabeth the regular questions—day, month, who sat in the Oval Office—to gauge her mental state she couldn't answer a single one. She moved her eyes and seemed to track the medics but the only clear answer she could give was a committed "no" when she was told they would be taking her to the hospital. Too bad for Elizabeth that choice was no longer hers.

The medics called the hospital and told them to be ready for a septic patient. Sepsis is taken as seriously as any other "code" be it not breathing or severe trauma. An infection had spread through Elizabeth's blood casting itself across her entire body. She was swimming in bacteria when she arrived at the hospital. A crew of doctors and nurses stood waiting for the ambulance to pull up. They sprung into action. Retaking vitals, running scans, pumping Elizabeth with enough antibiotics to kill an E. coli the size of a buffalo. It was like a scene from a medical drama, people running all around Elizabeth's body. It didn't take long for every drip to be started, every medicine to be pushed, every scan to be done. After that Elizabeth was wheeled into a curtained off area to wait for a bed to open up.

Five or fifteen hours later, one did. Elizabeth didn't notice what with her body filled to capacity with opioids and bacterial death. Once they found a room in the hospital Elizabeth was wheeled up there to wait; this time what she was waiting for was less clear. Mostly just waiting for the medical types to find a diagnosis to hang their hat on and admit to themselves and Elizabeth that there was nothing much they could do for her.

This process took longer than one would think. Elizabeth was out of it but there was no proof it was dementia. She was very frail and skinny but without doing batteries of invasive tests it was unclear if she had cancer or not. They could have done the tests but Elizabeth couldn't consent, as she had lost all ability to speak and communicate. There was no next of kin to authorize the test. The tests could have killed her anyway. After two days of waiting Elizabeth was diagnosed as "failure to thrive," meaning she was losing weight and ability and there was no clear understanding as to why. It seems that "thriving," at least in a technical medical sense, simply refers to eating and moving a little. "Thriving" is something like being able to scoot yourself onto a bedside commode and bring a spoon of pudding to your own face. A fairly low bar, but by this definition Elizabeth's infection was thriving even if she wasn't. Cancer and forest fires also thrive by this definition.

The time came for Elizabeth to get out of the hospital, but without a surrogate decision-maker that was tricky. Shockingly while the hospital didn't have the funds or resources to keep caring for Elizabeth, they were able to find the funds and resources to jump through the endless hoops and legal vagaries required to get Elizabeth "ward of the state" status. Being a "ward of the state" carried with it certain rights and benefits. Among those being that Elizabeth was put on Medicaid or she would after the state spent down what cash she had. After that, Medicaid dollars would pay for a long-term care facility.

The Gardens of Cambridge was the facility that the worker assigned to Elizabeth's case chose for Elizabeth to spend the rest of her life at. Perhaps unsurprisingly the Gardens was the facility that the social worker always went with. The Gardens of Cambridge had neither a garden (outside of a small cactus slowly dying on the front desk) nor was it located in Cambridge. The facility was actually in Downsburg, a much more apt name. Its beds were lined with this social worker's wards. There was no kickback, no scam, the facility wanted the Medicare patients, which represented an endless source of revenue and very little family members to deal with. Other facilities wanted private insurance or private pay patients that could be more lucrative, if a bigger hassle. The Gardens never said no to the social worker and as such this is where their caseload went. It also made it easy to visit everyone in a single day, which with a caseload like this social worker had was a necessity.

Elizabeth was transferred by ambulance, the EMT in the back with her spent the ride texting with an abusive boyfriend, which created tension in the back of the bus. Elizabeth may or may not have felt it, but it drew the EMTs attention. The ride was hard on Elizabeth's frail body, any change in homeostasis is hard on a dying body. The bumps in the road caused her pulse to spike. The EMT didn't really notice, wouldn't have done much, or couldn't have done all that much if she had. EMTs have a very limited scope of practice; Elizabeth's ride was basically an expensive and loud Uber.

Elizabeth arrived at the facility with a low oxygen level and high heart rate. She was placed in a bed in a room with two roommates that smelled awful. The EMTs, their job done, left without saying goodbye. They told the staff at the nurses' station that the new patient was "settling in." It would take until the start of the next shift before Elizabeth had "settled" or at least that long until anyone came to check on her. Elizabeth's medical needs were left to sit until an hour after that, when it was time to "pass meds." She was given seventeen medications in various forms. Each had been prescribed at the hospital. There were pills crushed in applesauce, liquid mediation, three patches on her skin, a spray up the nose, a fluid under the tongue, a couple regular pills, and four suppositories. The nurse got all this into Elizabeth in less than a minute, didn't even change gloves or wash her hands between Elizabeth and her roommates. The shift supervisor couldn't help but compliment this nurses' productivity and efficiency. She didn't get a raise for it but was able to put her feet up a couple minutes earlier.

Once properly medicated Elizabeth was not a problem. Outside of the occasional moan she could have been a large paperweight. A paperweight that was slowly breaking down into nothing. That was the goal really. Nobody would have said that and there really wasn't any intentional effort to turn Elizabeth from human to paperweight, but the system itself worked this twisted alchemy.

The transformation from human to paperweight may have begun with Elizabeth's illness but it was really pushed along by the medication. The doctors could have lowered the dose on some of the medications. If the doc had done this, there is a good chance Elizabeth would have woken up more, moved around more. And moving around more could have led to any number of issues. First Elizabeth might have fallen out of the bed. If she did, you're talking broken bones and bruises. Nursing homes don't care for either. There were rails on the bed designed to guard against this but they served more as obstacles for squirming patients to get around or get hung up on, causing all sorts of injuries. If an injury is bad enough it could lead to a hospitalization, and hospitalizations look bad and bring lawsuits. Lawsuits cost money, so better to let the chemicals restrict Elizabeth to her bed. A knocked out patient doesn't have all that many issues.

On top of falling out of bed if Elizabeth were to wake up she might eventually understand where she was. Or more likely become aware of her own helplessness. She might want someone to take her to the bathroom. Or she might want to take a shower. Maybe she would just want some company. Elizabeth might eventually find the pull cord that buzzed the staff's pagers. The state requires these pull cords and once every few years checked to make sure they worked. Staff at nursing facilities hate pull cords and pagers. The little buzzing demands hooked onto the top of their scrubs, constantly urging them to some new and ghastly situation.

When a patient, who can pull a cord, got their hands on one, all hell would break loose. They might use it correctly, they might only pull the cord when they need to. If it were used the way intended it might even be a helpful thing. It might help the nursing staff avoid simple problems that could get out of hand and make more work for them. That said, some patients are known to "hang on" the cord. Pulling on the electric summons for every slight inconvenience like horrible pain, terror, a wet or filthy bed, a need for human interaction. That or terrible, terrible hunger pains. A confused person may simply pull on a cord because it's a cord to pull on. The Gardens was staffed with one aide to fifty patients. They simply did not have the time or energy to deal with such minor issues. There was laundry to be done, meals to be set in front of people who would never eat them, and endless, pointless paperwork to be filled out, unread, and put away until such time has passed that the papers could be deleted or shredded.

There were ways to deal with patients who chronically "hang on" the cord that didn't involve massive amounts of drugs. This was usually done by hiding the cord or pushing the bed out of reach. These techniques worked well but could really upset the odd family member who might show up to visit their loved one. The one thing that could be done that would work for everyone, make the least waves, and avoid the most lawsuits was to dope them up.

The same logic exists for those patients who don't pull on the cord but instead shout. The boss doesn't care for hearing screaming patients up and down the halls. It's a bad look, but a look that couldn't be all the way avoided, not totally. There is a reason people are removed from society and "placed" in the Gardens and facilities like it. They are places designed for people to suffer at, away from the rest of us. The suffering there can get loud once in a while, an ancient instinct to call for help when you're in pain. If this instinct became disruptive, as it often did, for staff and visitors and government regulators, then medications could be used to end that disruption.

Elizabeth, every so often, would find her way through the haze and into the real world. It was a world she didn't recognize. A world populated by two breathing corpses, one on either side of her. A world filled with strange sounds and smells. A world both too hot and too cold. Too hot in the summer because the AC was always on the fritz; too cold in the winter because the only way to deal with the overactive boiler was to open the windows, letting the frigid air mix with the radiator steam. While Elizabeth never fully came to herself in these moments she did become aware of this strange out-of-place sensation. What she touched and smelled, saw, heard, tasted— all were foreign. Unknown and unpleasant, and these sensations were her entire world. As this realization rose near to the level of consciousness Elizabeth did what any reasonable and rational person would do. She screamed.

The terror of this strange new world filled her up from her toes to her head and exited through her mouth. Her screams were a sound both horrible and normal in the place she found herself. Even terror can become mundane when it's ubiquitous. This screaming, the Gardens of Cambridge couldn't have it. The doctor under whose medical license the place operated even though she only stopped in once a month was informed of the screaming. The aide complained to the nurse, the nurse to the manager, the manager to the executive, the executive to the doctor. Nobody besides the aide had actually heard the screaming, which was a good thing as it meant hopefully none of the other patients, aside from Elizabeth's two-sided roommates or any visiting families, had heard it either.

The doctor immediately, without seeing Elizabeth, prescribed a massive dose of Seroquel. Seroquel is an antipsychotic drug that has a sedative effect. The perfect medication for addressing Elizabeth's (entirely reasonable given the situation she found herself in) disruptive screaming. The drug was administered in such a dose that little of Elizabeth remained. Making life much easier for staff, administration, and visitors.

Elizabeth was now the fleshy paperweight everyone hoped and knew she could become. Put food in, clean what comes out when you can, cash the check from the state. Her new world had reached equilibrium and perfect efficiency. But there is a reason they make paperweights out of metal or stone or glass; those materials don't wear down easily; bodies do. It didn't take long for the bedbound Elizabeth to become full of holes and new infections. The infections were treated aggressively with antibiotics, the holes largely just covered and left to fester. People can hurt, they can fall apart, it doesn't matter. It was decided for Elizabeth that what mattered most for her was perfusion, that the machinations of life continue for as long as possible. All life being equally billable by the facility. Keeping the flesh alive until it becomes too burdensome to do so, that can take a while.

Elizabeth would never talk again, never laugh or dance or sing again. She would never verbalize a coherent thought, tell a joke or laugh at one. These basic activities were no longer part of Elizabeth's life. She would lay, defecate, hurt, occasionally moan. She would take her nutrition through a feeding tube. The only taste she would know was the acrid bile in the back of her throat when they gave her more nutrition than her broken body could process.

The Gardens were good at turning people into paperweights; it was what they knew and what they did. They were less a nursing facility and more a flesh paperweight factory. What the management didn't expect was that Elizabeth was known to tip the old elbow once in a while if a "while" is every single day. When Elizabeth worked, she'd have an eye opener to start the day, a tipple in the afternoon. Elizabeth and her mom would polish off a couple of bottles of wine every night, with Elizabeth enjoying the lion's share of the grape.

The drinking continued once Elizabeth stopped working. She pretty much had a cocktail in hand bell to bell. She rarely got hammered, her habit was more like a pilot light of booze, always pouring out but never too much. Most people that knew Elizabeth had no idea she even touched the stuff. Once in a while Elizabeth would forget to pick up her booze. This wasn't a problem as she would always dip a little bit into her mom's medication. Morphine tended to act a hell of a lot quicker than vino. Elizabeth could never really down booze, and would never dream of stooping so low as to buy drugs off the street. But a nip from her ma's medicine bottle didn't seem too bad. They were related anyway, what was hers was mom's and what was mom's was hers. If her mom could handle the morphine Elizabeth could too.

This went on for years with Elizabeth taking more and more as her tolerance grew. The doctor never questioned it when Elizabeth asked for more meds. Sweet little old lady was in pain, what's a little more juice of the poppy? You'd think they were getting paid to dispense the stuff. Nobody ever found out about Elizabeth's problem. Once her mother was gone it wasn't anything really for her to ask the doctor for some more of the good stuff. Who was he to say no? If he asked, she had back pain from caring for her mother, or carpal tunnel from her years in the office. They seemed like reasonable sources of pain, and as the doctor had been told pain needed to be medicated. What could go wrong?

Elizabeth enjoyed rural Ohio amounts of opioids all on the dime of her insurance company. Elizabeth had a prescription; she picked up the drugs in a clean, well-lit pharmacy in front of all her neighbors. She never thought she had a problem. And since her primary doctor had given up her case when Elizabeth moved into the Gardens, her medication history didn't follow her to her new home.

What this meant was that the facility staff and medical director were completely unaware of the fact that Elizabeth could handle more heroin than Andy Warhol. She was what was medically known as opioid experienced. As such the medications that worked fine at first began to work less and less. Elizabeth began calling out again, first moans and yelps but then the most dreaded word. The word that people couldn't just pass by.

This most dreaded word wasn't "fire," as one might think, though that word caused its own set of problems. "Fire" is something that could affect the hearer. It means that the passerby could be in danger, after all the Gardens was full of oxygen tanks. Combine that with fire and the problems of the dying become everyone's problem. It's good for the nursing home that people very, very rarely call out "fire."

Elizabeth didn't call out the second worst word she could call out from management's perspective, that word being "help." "Help" is the second worst word for a patient to call out as it makes a request, sometimes a demand on those poor souls who just happen to be strolling the hallway. "Help" is hard to ignore.

That said, "help" can be ignored. It's not comfortable to ignore, but it can be. We have to learn to ignore people's calls for help. We ignore cries for help made by the homeless on the street. We convince ourselves that they don't actually need our help, that all these people on street corners are actually rich and when they leave their corners they walk back down the street to their BMWs, hop in, and take a ride back to their penthouse apartments. Once comfy in their digs they fill bathtubs with our filthy loose change and crumbled bills, and swim around like Scrooge McDuck. With this in mind we can ignore when they ask for help.

We are conditioned to tune out the cries of those in need because it might get us in trouble. We might pick a guy out of a ditch only to get sued for pulling on their arm too hard. Or we might hear a person crying out for help as they are getting attacked and worry that if we get involved we might get hurt. Of these scenarios, the rich homeless, the litigious injured, the crime that gets turned on us, they are all well-documented and told to us over and over again by friends and family and a media who seem to prefer that nobody ever lends a hand, no matter how rarely these things actually occur. When someone asks for help 999 times out of 1,000 they actually need it, or at least could use it. Still these stories of exceptions give us pause and numb us to the needs of others. Over time we can pass by the bed of a patient calling out "help" inoculated from their pain by the world around us, and the twenty other patients calling out the same.

But Elizabeth didn't call out "help" from her hospital bed, she called out the word that the management of the Gardens and every other nursing facility hate to hear most. She called out "mommy," and even worse the horrible, terrifying, "mommy help." This was too much for the powers that be. "Fire" was rare, "help" easy to ignore, but "mommy." One couldn't deny the humanity of someone who calls that word out from the depths of pain and sorrow.

When an adult calls for their mommy it tugs on the hearer's heart-strings. What's more human than a person calling for their mommy. Dogs and cats have parents or parentage. Bees have queens, single cell organisms split from other single cell organisms, but only humans have mommies. A paperweight doesn't have a mommy at all. One way or another all humans have called out for their mommies to feed and protect them when they couldn't feed or protect themselves. Hearing a voice call out for mommy calls back to the helplessness of childhood.

We take away the humanity of the old and sick but kids are the most human of all of us. We don't put away sick children, we draw them near. We tell their stories. A child remains a human even when terminal. Hearing a person, even an old and sick person way past their humanity, call out "mommy" reminds the hearer that the old person comes from the same stuff as them. That though a person has lost their faculties and functionality, they remain human—no matter how hard we hide that fact from ourselves.

When someone passed by Elizabeth's room and heard the doped up and dying woman call out "mommy," many were stirred to action. The facility hated when visitors got stirred to action. This action usually amounted to pacing around the nurses' station nervously. First waiting to see a nurse at all, which could take some time, often enough for them to give up. If there was a nurse at the nurses' station the next task became the Herculean effort of getting their attention. There are stories of monasteries that will make a seeker of enlightenment wait outside the doors on some mountain top, cold and wet and starving before allowing them access to spiritual training. These monks had less ability to ignore those seekers in the cold than did the nurses at the Gardens. A person could stand at the station patiently bleeding to death and never get so much as a hello.

The vast majority of the time even a patient calling out "mommy" ends there, with a person waiting at the nurses' station long enough that they feel they have done their duty. But one day Elizabeth's shouts drew the attention of the wrong kind of visitor. This particular visitor happened to be a member of a local church. She had signed up to deliver communion to church members and other Catholics at the facility. It was this volunteer's first day on the job. She had recently retired from a major leadership role at a large corporation. She was a forceful person, wildly successful in business, so successful that she retired at sixty. However, two months into retirement she found herself bored as can be. So when the priest asked for volunteers during announcements after Sunday service this woman jumped at the opportunity to lend a hand. Not only was this woman successful in business but she also grew up wealthy and as such hadn't spent time in facilities like the Gardens. That was by design as these places didn't want people with power getting a look at how they operate. Those types, who had time and money and were used to getting their own way, could be a real headache for places like the Gardens. But what reason would someone from money and privilege have for going to the Gardens? Their loved ones had private caregivers or lived in fancy assisted living facilities. The Gardens was an ugly building they drove by, they saw the ambulance parked at, their communities received taxes from, but they were not places they visited. This woman was an outlier and the management was not fond of outliers.

The volunteer heard Elizabeth call out while passing by the room. Unsure and sheepish, the volunteer looked in the room. Elizabeth was moving uncomfortably in the bed. She had foam boots on her feet to prevent her heels from rubbing together, causing sores. Elizabeth was gaunt, slightly yellow, and dying. The volunteer entered the room slowly, drawn by the siren song of Elizabeth's terrified screams, and inched toward the bed. Elizabeth reached out with one skeletal hand. The volunteer wasn't sure if Elizabeth was reaching for her, or something else, or nothing at all. Instinctively the volunteer stepped back, but she didn't leave. The volunteer pulled up the slightly soiled vinyl chair from the corner of the room. She had to brush off the various nightgowns, foam wedges, and discarded medical packaging that had been stacked on the chair. She brushed dust off the chair so thick it made her cough. The volunteer pulled the chair up and sat with Elizabeth. After a while of sitting and holding Elizabeth's hand, the volunteer thought Elizabeth had calmed down. She got up to leave, but Elizabeth squeezed the volunteer's hand hard, digging her nails into the soft flesh. Her eyes opened for the first time looking wildly in the volunteer's direction. "Mommy" she shouted.

The volunteer tried telling Elizabeth it was going to be "okay." Though there was no possible scenario in which what she was experiencing was going to be "okay." The volunteer looked around the room for some kind of help. All she found was two other human paperweights in their beds, silent and unmoving. The volunteer looked back at her hand and felt a little sick, and tried to gently extract once more. This only made Elizabeth squeeze tighter and again call out "mommy." The volunteer tried harder to remove her hand. Elizabeth's uncut filthy nails were now leaving thick impressions on the back of the volunteer's hand. Elizabeth's eyes grew large again, "mommy" she nearly screamed.

This was too much for the volunteer who peeled back Elizabeth's claw-like grip. The volunteer stood up, pushing the chair back with her legs, never taking her eyes off Elizabeth. Elizabeth on the other hand had shut her eyes tight and continued to scream "mommy" with growing urgency. The volunteer backed away from Elizabeth, slowly as though she were backing away from a grizzly bear, keeping her eyes on Elizabeth until she was well clear of the door. Once around the corner the volunteer made a beeline for the nurses' station.

She had time, money, and an injured conscience, not what management wanted to deal with. The nursing staff tried their usual methods, but the volunteer wouldn't be ignored or placated. She wanted something done, if not she would never have gotten to sleep that night. And she wanted to see it done with her own eyes.

It took a while for a nurse to realize how serious the situation was. In all honesty the volunteer may have given up but Elizabeth's call of "mommy" kept on coming from down the hall, burrowing its way into the volunteer's skull. A tell-tale heart of dying screams pulsing in the back of the volunteer's brain.

Eventually, after standing at the desk for twenty minutes listening to Elizabeth from down the hall, after multiple threats to reach out to the manager, a nurse agreed to go and give Elizabeth some medication. It took some time for the massive quantity of sedative to kick in but eventually it did its job, leaving Elizabeth silent and allowing the volunteer to go home knowing she had done her good deed for the day. She slept like a baby that night, but never returned to the Gardens. The patients there would have to get the body of Christ someplace else.

The medication would work this time, the management made sure of it. "As needed" medications were now given regularly. Milligrams were doubled, times given per day were expanded. The goal was not pain medication, it wasn't to keep Elizabeth in bed, it wasn't to deal with anxiety. The goal was to make sure that Elizabeth never called out to her mother again. It worked and the already weak Elizabeth got weaker. Lack of motion and the slow poisoning of the medications themselves wore her down. Eventually something happened that happens to many bodies allowed to slowly deteriorate. Elizabeth lost the ability to swallow her own mucus or clear her own secretions. This creates the sound known as the death rattle. The death rattle was the last sound that Elizabeth would ever make, and it was quiet enough that nobody really noticed, not even her roommates. Or if they did they were keeping it pretty close to the chest. That's how they found her one morning. Dead and cold in bed, a stream of viscous fluid slowly draining from Elizabeth's open mouth. All the nurse could say was, "She has suffered enough."

Elizabeth's stay at the Gardens was by no means a strange event.

Interlude

Mommy, Mommy, Why Have You Forsaken Me?

ELIJAH'S HONEY

Once, it was a forerunner. If you'll have it, a prophet. Appearing. An announcement. Of the imminence. Of the coming. Of that great and glorious night. Then, like all whose fires burn loudly, it was disappeared. Taken down. Or, more likely, stolen. And with pride. Scotch-taped. Elevated pulse. To adolescent walls. Memories of hope fulfilled. A room saturated with life.

But that was a long time ago. Today these walls greet guests with heavy eyes. Silent. Jaundiced. Toward a bedpan slouching. The space between them has taken to gorging itself. Frequently. Chocolate and candy corn. Boxes and bookends. Willing or otherwise. Victims of exhaustion and swift declutterings.

That flier? Again, it's gone.

Though it's been years since the final strum of the final G, amps unplugged, butts and bottles swept from drains, even in its absence, something of the foreshadow of the fruition of this prophet's announcement remains. Here. On the door of a church. Clinging steadfastly as *goo*. Hardened. Gaunt. Rectangular. In its isolation, it, too, has become a collector. Not of life's heavy things. It is weak. But of dust. And of dander. And of atmospheric things.

Invisible to most. Insignificant to more, its very existence, nonetheless, is a gesture. Pointing toward and participating in that which lies beyond. For those who have hearts to receive:

Elation. Exhilaration. Satiation.

Home.

The invocation of a memory of a moment divine.

The goo on the door? Just goo.

That's all it is.

And also:

so much more.

THE CHILD LEAPT

Beneath each prayer, each dream, each hunch, each premonition toward a better world or a better life, there is a ghost. Dwelling. Between gut and heart. Wrapped tight in the traffic jam of nerves we call the solar plexus. The place from which our wind gets knocked. And the place from which our prayers depart.

It is there, prophetic *goo* clung in desperation to a church door in anticipation of something (perhaps) salvific, that this ghost *slimes* each wish. Each hunger. Each hope. Each hunch. Each prophetic proclamation and prayer that passes by, rising from the pain that furnishes our depths and stretches toward the desert skies.

IT SHALL BE CALLED

Once, decades ago, a poet who was courageous (if not deranged) decided to give this ghost a name. He named it after a dynamic and multi-emotional internal phenomenon that, against all odds, came to find a home in the language called Portuguese. Brazilians (like this poet) and other speakers of this language to this day swear even to their most vengeful gods that there is no word like it. At all. Not in any language. Not in any world. It is unique.[1]

And so it is with our ghost—who, rather than haunting through regressive narrative loops of unresolved traumas and unrequited loves (as most ghosts are known to do), a needle a-skip and a-skip, haunts, instead, by way of an evocation, a conjuring, a summoning *forward*, into the reality that yet another poet (and mystic) has named the Not Yet.[2]

"The presence of an absence."

1. Alves, *Transparencies of Eternity*, 15.
2. Bloch, *Principle of Hope*, 56.

"A piece of me wrenched out of me."

"Cleaning up the room of a child who has died."[3]

"And Yet. . . ." "And Yet!"

"Not Yet, and Yet. . . ."[4]

These words express the emotional internal phenomenon called Saudade.[5]

And so this is the name that the poet gave to our ghost.

OH, HOLY & PRODIGAL

Our ghost is older than the *goo*, and younger than you and me. Its birth, announced at our first frustration. There, we cried out in protest, fists raised, announcing our demands. We had seen Paradise. We had tasted its *good*. Then, in a moment, it was all ripped away.

Let me explain.

Crossing the wilderness, we arrived in this world, compass a-spin, sucking at the sky, presuming (perhaps) that there might be life on this, the *other side*. Then, life arrived. Quickly. Running to us, open arms. Approaching us even while we were still far away. Ready with a banquet to celebrate and a fatted calf to slay. The Land of Milk was *at hand*. And we partook. And in partaking, there was pleasure. And there was sustenance. And there was *home*. Oh! There was *home*! All at once. All at the same time.[6]

Truly. We had arrived.

And there was much rejoicing in the presence of the angels of God.

NO PLACE TO REST

Then, Mother left. To the bathroom. To breakfast. To rest. To the clouds. To the sun. And where there was once a provision of milky bliss, there was now an absence.[7] *It's a ghost!* the doctor screamed smacking Saudade's behind. *Congratulations! Congratulations! You each have a twin!*

---

3. Alves, *Transparencies of Eternity*, 15.

4. Puelo, "Rubem Alves," 190–91.

5. Alves, *Transparencies of Eternity*, 15.

6. Alves, *Poet*, 70–77.

7. Alves, *Poet*, 27–28.

And so it was that, in the form of desire, in the form of nauseous longing, in the form of hungry hope in the presence of an absence, at our first voice and void, Saudade arrived, clinging to our Paradise lost, finding warmth and belonging in our first splanchnic twist.

HOSANNAS

Saudade: the ghost who haunts each desire, each prayer, each dream. The clear coat sealing that embraces each eschatological anticipation, each longing for utopias, heavens, and homes, and every heart and tongue afire. The *goo* that clings desperately to each eager yearning (At last! At last!): for a *parousia*, no longer delayed: for an entry triumphal, coats and palms returned to the earth.

> Our own beloved:
> Mother.
> Death.

WHO DO YOU SAY THAT I AM?

Goo. The residue of a memory of a feeling of a time once had. Pleasure. Elation. Exhilaration. Sustenance. Satiation. Home. The presence of an absence giving birth to a ghost. The presence of an absence giving birth to crying and protestation and hope.

> Songs in a prisoner's cell.
> Screams as earthquakes in nursing home halls:
> quickening the dead
> stirring the staff half alive
> shaking the art from the walls.

STREPITUS

Mommy, Mommy!
> Why have you forsaken me?
> Mommy, Mommy!
> I thirst.
> Mommy, Mommy!
> I cannot save myself.

Child, behold your Mother!
Into your hands, I give my ghost.

IT IS FINISHED

For they know not.
   Silence.

ASCENSION

Beneath each prayer, each dream, each hunch, each premonition,
   there is a ghost.
   And she is seated at the right hand of the mother.

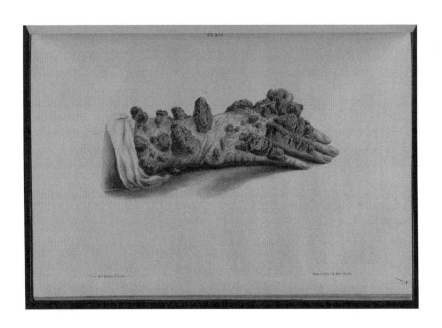

CHAPTER FOUR

Mik the Worm King

When Micky was around people put the fine china away. He was wild, a cyclone of energy and activity. He couldn't help it, and it caused him trouble, especially at school. His folks had adjusted early to the energy; they didn't have a choice. They gave him impossible jobs to tire him out. Digging holes to China in the backyard, running laps around the block, hunting snipes. Most people thought snipes were fictional rodents, but in reality they are living, breathing, flying birds. His days were spent on fool's errands and wild goose chases. His nights were spent restless in bed, or out of bed.

In the mornings Mik's family would find their house turned upside down. Sometimes in the deep darkness Mik would decide to rearrange the furniture, or make root beer floats for the family. The detritus left behind after such activity would be found scattered throughout the home. His folks were weary, the dog confused, the cat, well the cat was indifferent, and the goldfish stayed up at night praying Mik wouldn't decide to give her a bath. It was a tough time. It was also just before the advent of medication that could conveniently tamp down these impulses in the child, and his parents were too kind to beat him, not that it would have worked anyway.

His teachers complained endlessly, made him write "I will sit still" on the chalkboard hundreds of times. Had him sit in the back of the class facing the wall. Mik practically had his own key to the principal's office but nothing worked. They knew Mik was a sweet kid, they knew he didn't want to cause trouble; he simply couldn't help himself. Everything came to a head when Mik was practicing for the school musical.

His folks thought the musical would be a great idea, that the kid would burn off some of that endless energy singing and dancing. Micky took to it, as he took to everything. The problem was he took to it a little too hard. The kid wouldn't stop singing everywhere he went, and the music teacher had ambitiously chosen *Cats* that year, which didn't help. Mik's teacher told him that if she heard him sing the word "jellicle" just one more time in class he would be sent home for the day; his parents had told him if they heard the word "jellicle" one more time they would send him off with the circus. He tried to be quiet. When that didn't work he tried just to hum, but not half an hour into second period when everyone was silently working on their times tables, Mik belted, "Old Deuteronomy married nine wives and more I am tempted to say ninety-nine." He caught himself after that but it was too late, the damage was done. How could he help it? Jellicles are and jellicles do; his parents retrieved him from the principal's office.

They let him run ahead on the walk home. Since they had the afternoon free due to Mik dragging them from their work to pick him up they decided to take the long way through the woods. That morning it had poured down, but now the world was in the strange calm between the storm and the sun. A few stray drips from the morning rain fell on the family but light broke through the clearing sky. Mik ran ahead, his folks walked behind wondering what to do with him. They were lost in their worried conversation, not paying attention to the kid who had finally gone silent. Which was great because he was approaching "Memory" in the song bill for *Cats*, and earnest as he was, the kid just didn't have the pipes. Micky had become so silent in fact that his parents almost tripped over the kid.

The rain had drawn out the worms. The creatures littered the paved path through the woods. Hundreds of squirmy worms curled up and spread out all along the trail. Mik knew that some wouldn't make it. He had seen the sidewalks after a storm, the horror of gelatinous bodies strewn about. Left to dry. It broke the kid's heart every time. So he was saving them.

One by one Mik crouched down, picked the wiggling worms up off the trail and gently set them in the grass. He seemed to have lost all touch with the world around him. Mik's eyes were on the pavement, scanning, searching. The rain had brought down twigs and leaves. Mik separated the sticks from the worms. They looked surprisingly similar. Little by little Mik made his way forward, but it was slow going; there were many worms to be saved.

His folks watched for a while in stunned silence. Finally, his father spoke up, "Okay now Micky cut it out we need to get home." Micky looked up at his old man, eyes filled with tears.

"Dad, how can I save this one and not the next?" Mik asked, crouching down for the next worm. Micky's parents just looked at each other. The walk to get home should have taken five minutes, they were on the trail for over an hour.

When they got home, Mik sat down quietly and did what homework they gave a first grader, he looked at a picture book for a while. He ate a good quarter of his dinner and drank a cup of milk. The family sat and watched some TV together, he brushed his teeth and went to sleep. He slept like a rock.

Things were better the next few days. It was April and it was getting warmer. The family was happy to be out of the house in the early spring sun. Mik was busy in the backyard, and since the day on the trail he hadn't been in much trouble at school or at home. Calm rested on the land, but when there is calm we know what comes next. It being April, it wasn't long until the rains tore through town.

It was about two weeks after the walk home when the rains came again. They came every day for two weeks. Each morning the waters of heaven pummeled the earth below, and each day between 2 and 5 p.m. the rain would stop. Micky waited by the back door on these days. He looked nervous and anxious. The child who could be distracted by anything, from a blue car to a pair of shiny keys, was perfectly focused on the sidewalk.

The instant the rain had stopped, Mik was out the door. Dad or Mom trailed along behind. One by one he gently, sweetly, like a mother with a newborn, picked up the creatures and put them back in the grass. Mom worried about his catching a cold, Dad about salmonella, both about what the neighbors might say. At first they had tried to dissuade their son from his task. They reminded him that worms were ugly and slimy. They tried to argue that it was simply too much; there were too many worms. They had tried just telling him "no" but when they did he would sit at the door staring out at the sidewalk, whimpering. A horrible sound, hard to describe. Something beyond sorrow; the sound God must make looking down at our world and seeing what we're doing with the place.

"How can I save one and not save the next," was Micky's refrain when asked why he was doing what he was doing. That was that. Every rain storm they took him out. For the entire year and on to the next. It got easier as he grew larger. His parents didn't have to follow him around with an umbrella, but instead handed him a raincoat and let him go out on his own. Mik became known around the neighborhood. Some of the neighbors were touched by the sentiment of his worm-saving activity. They would cheer him on, or talk about how nice their gardens looked because the worms he was saving were turning the soil. Maybe it was just the spring rains, but it was true that the neighborhood lawns and vegetable plots had never looked better.

The kids weren't so nice, or not all of them. Some treated Mik like he had a problem of sorts, an issue that led to his compulsion. Maybe they were right, but Mik didn't want the pity that came with it. Others were just mean, hence the name Mik the Worm King. A name that would follow him around the rest of his life. His parents thought he might grow out of it, that as he got older some new obsession would take over, a sport or girls or something. Both of those definitely came into his mind, both of those he cared about the same as any other kid his age, along with other things, but the worms would not go away. Every storm Mik was out the door, saving the worms. "How can I save one and not the next?"

His parents didn't know what to do. They considered moving to a drier climate that might have less worms, maybe out in the desert or something, but scorpions and armadillos might cause them more trouble, so they decided to stay the course, as did the worms.

Micky lived as normal a life as he could, as any neighborhood weirdo could. From the bird man who fed the pigeons during the day and in the night scrubbed himself clean. Or the burlap sack guy, whose wardrobe left something to be desired and little to the imagination. Or the street preachers, and the guy who pedals around his cart sharpening knives. Mik, even as a child, joined the ranks of the eccentric and the odd, not by choice but as a refugee. He did okay in school. That is he managed to graduate. He was held back once and some kind-hearted teachers might have let him through when they really shouldn't have. He also took a few "special" classes, but most of his studies were done right along with the other kids. On days when it rained they just let him out of class. Some teachers were resistant to this at first, not wanting to indulge the kid's habit, but then they watched the physical torture and mental anguish that seemed to consume him when he was stuck indoors. With the squirming and the tears, eventually even the hardest of asses gave way and let him go.

Mik's social life dried up like a worm on the sidewalk. While the town's gardens bloomed, any hope of friendship or romance withered. Nobody wanted to be associated with the "Worm King." Mik's best friends growing up were his parents, but he seemed okay with that. When school was over he got a job down at the local garden center. It was a hopping joint, the village was named "Best Gardens in the State" a decade straight. It created a kind of civic pride, which fed on itself. As such the garden center was one of the happiest places in town. Mr. Brown the owner knew he owed a debt of gratitude to Mother Teresa for the worms and as such was more than happy to hire Mik on. Mr. Brown was even willing to indulge Micky on his worm hunts if it should rain on his shift, provided he put the worms in a can and brought them back to the garden center to turn the compost.

It went on like this for years. Mik went to work everyday, and when it was over he came home. Besides the worms he had a few hobbies. He liked old TV, especially *The Three Stooges* and *Batman*. He was a big fan of professional wrestling. Once a year Mik and his folks would spend a week up at the lake. Mik would wander the trails in the woods and swim in the lake. For a guy committed to saving the worms he loved to fish, though he always threw them back with a heartfelt apology.

He had no real relationships outside of his parents. Sure he was friendly with his boss, and famous around town, but nobody came by the house. No birthday parties, no bowling league. It was a simple life, but he never missed a rain storm. He never left the worms to die. The gardens grew and the worms survived. Mik got older and so did his parents.

Mik's dad died first, as father's tend to do. He was about five years into retirement when a grabber ended him up in the hospital, and an infection made sure he never would leave. Mik and his cousins carried the casket. He didn't like the black suit, and as they were carrying the body to the grave it began to rain. It took everything he had not to set the casket down and look for worms. Mik and his mom missed the repast to wander the windy streets of the cemetery fulfilling Micky's calling. Neither Mik nor his mother minded much. They didn't speak at all. Mik working, his mother watching. At one point, she bent down, the hem of her dress dragging on the wet pavement and picked up a worm herself. She didn't like the slime but there was something satisfying in the action.

From there a new routine set in. Mik took on some of his father's responsibilities around the house. Doing various tasks, maintaining the yard, cleaning, shoveling the steps. Mik and his mother were constant companions except when Mik was at work. She would indulge her son watching hour after hour of old *Batman* reruns, *The Green Hornet*, and whatever else happened to pique his interest. She did the cooking, something she had loved to do her whole life. It got simpler though as she aged and struggled with the heavy pots and pans. Eventually she had to chop veggies on a cutting board at her rocking chair, as standing for long periods had become impossible. Eventually Mik took over the cooking duties as well.

He didn't mind cooking, though the menu did become much more limited. Mik's dad's pension was a life preserver not a pleasure yacht. They got by as well they could, the little money Mik brought in was enough given their situation. The house was paid off; Micky's dad had bought the place on the GI Bill ages ago. Most of the appliances were original, and as such would stand the test of time. They had an old station wagon, the same one that had lugged them up to the lake every year. If it was raining Micky's mom might drive it to the grocery store; Micky never did get his license. They lived together this way for decades. Micky's mom slowly getting sicker, and Micky devoting himself more and more to her care.

That burden weighed heavier and heavier on Mik. The tasks required to care for mom were growing in difficulty and in skill level and importance. He had to help her walk from one room to the next. Her on a walker, Micky trailing behind with a wheelchair in case she fell. Eventually he had to help her in the bathroom. That was hard on both at first, but embarrassment will always give way to necessity. Then it was the shower, which was more difficult and higher stakes. One afternoon she slipped and Micky wasn't quick enough to catch her. Micky couldn't get her up. When the paramedics arrived she was shivering in the tub, Micky next to her desperately trying to dry her off, a pile of towels stacked on top of her and dripping next to the tub. Nothing was broken but she had bruises that ran the entire side of her body. After her hospital stay, Micky's mom went to rehab for ninety days. For the first time since he was a kid the Worm King couldn't sleep. Scared to be alone, the fifty-five year old man missed his mommy.

On the day she died it rained. Micky was out saving worms when it happened. She may have waited for that moment to die. Waited for Micky to be doing that which defined him, that which seemed to give him peace. At least he could have that moment before he found her. She could take her rest knowing he was in his element. She had been waiting to die. Micky had been avoiding thinking about it, maybe he couldn't think about it. His mom wasn't alone, after rehab, when a mass was discovered spinning itself through her body. Micky's mom was sent home on hospice. A caregiver was with her when she breathed her last. When Micky got home he found his Ma in bed; the caregiver had cleaned her up, even put on makeup and necklaces that she used to wear to church, but only on Easter. Mik climbed into bed with his mother, and laid there for three hours until the funeral home arrived. Once they had taken her away, he got back in that bed and didn't move until the next morning.

After his mom passed Micky let a lot of things go. He missed work, which was unlike him. His boss was patient with him to a fault, but even he had his limits and eventually he had to let Mik go. Without his job, or his Ma, all that Mik had left was the worms. He survived, and that's about it. Micky became disheveled, a huge shock of graying hair, giant beard, threadbare clothes. Neighborhood kids made up legends about the man. He was a villain, leading unsuspecting victims to his house, where he fed them to his pit of worms.

His mother had saved money for him. The hospice social worker had worked with her to get meals on wheels set up for Micky. He owned the home outright, had a couple bucks in an account his mother had left for him. That along with Social Security was enough to provide for his needs, but not much more.

The house fell into disrepair. Outside of the storms Micky was rarely seen outside the house. He sat inside watching classic TV shows. Some people stopped by to check on him. The same nagging church folks that his mother used to talk to at Sunday service. They never came in, just knocked and said "hello." Interesting that people only seemed to stop by Micky the Worm King's house when they were on their way to someplace else. Anyway it's good they did because one day he didn't answer. They found him in the bathroom. He slipped getting out of the tub and hit his head.

Micky was confused and dehydrated at the hospital. It didn't take more than a few IV bags, a couple of meals, and some amount of interaction with other human beings to get Micky back on his feet again. The hardest part of his stay was when he couldn't go out after a storm. He tried to, walking down the hall with his IV and hospital gown open for the world to see, ratty old whitey-tighties swinging in the wind. But the nursing staff stopped him and forced him back into his room. He screamed, they called security, medicine was given and that was that.

When it came time for him to go home, which was a few days later than he originally would have been released because of his run-in with security, Micky was sent home with some help. A caregiver was set up to come in every day to keep an eye on Mik. The doctors wanted to send him to a nursing home, but Micky wasn't having it; he couldn't let the worms die and he knew a place like that wouldn't let him out to do his thing. So the caregiver was put in place.

Mario was born in Manila. He had been in the US for a decade or so. He had been a nurse at home; he was a nurse's aide here. Mario liked Mik right away. The gentle Worm King was always appreciative, did what was asked, never complained. He only had one quirk: his endless quest to save the worms. At first Mario tried to keep Mik in the house after the storms, afraid he would get sick. But watching the man at the window looking out on the world, tears in his eyes, Mario couldn't take it. Soon enough Micky was again a staple on the street, only now he had Mario behind him. Micky would walk with a walker, Mario pushing a wheelchair in case Mik got dizzy or needed to sit down. Mario helping Mik, Mik helping the worms. One day a passerby, new to town, asked Mario what they were doing. Mario said, "How can he save one worm and not the next?"

Life went on like this for some time. Eventually Micky needed so much help that Mario moved into the house. Micky slept in his parents' bed, and Mario slept in Micky's room, still decorated with baseballs and cowboys. They watched old movies, saved worms, ate, and slept. Until one day, they must have gone out when it was too damp or too cold. That or maybe it was just bad luck. Micky caught a cold, and that cold became pneumonia. Micky ended up in the hospital; Mario came to visit. The doctors found Micky had some other previously undiagnosed health issues underlying his current illness. That and he picked up a nasty infection at the hospital. A month in the building, a week on vent, and Micky the Worm King died. Mario, Micky's old boss, and a couple of church people came to his funeral. He went from infamous to nightmare among the neighborhood kids, his ghost still haunting the night prowling for worm food. The lawns around town all turned brown.

Interlude

Go and Show Yourself to the Priests

It didn't take much to read the writing on the wall. A finicky switch. A hot light. A fan's drunken buzz. A mirror. And a transparency.

Transparencies were sheets, thin and made of plastic. At times, they came in a roll. On them, a teacher, an instructor, an artist, an engineer, a mathematician, a lyric-loving praise band groupie, was able to write—or print, or draw, or smudge—examples, illustrations, analytics, iterations, or ecstasies, as they were dreamt, spoken, solved, stewed-upon, or sung.

And there they would shine. Transfigured.

Perpendicular from that place where they were laid.

For Belshazzar and everyone to see.

Before transparencies, there were other ways to share with light. The slide show. A magic lantern. The camera obscura. Shadow play, magic mirrors, trotting horse lamps, and Pythagoras, with Heinrich Cornelius Agrippa, looking-glass in hand, inscribing magic blood-scripts onto the moon.[1]

The desire for one to have one's beautiful insides illuminate a room full of eager eyes is not a modern one, alone.

This is what we do. We shine our beauty for the world to see. And when we can't shine it, we share it, wearing it on buttons and on our sleeves.

And what do we do with that, within, which doesn't sparkle? Those things for which we've built cages in the forgotten oubliettes below? Those desolate and deserted parts where the perennial heads of the Baptists and the empty chairs of Elijahs are stored?

These we shine differently.

1. Pythagoras claimed to be able to write on the moon through a form of "projection" involving blood, magic, and glass. Shi, *Who's Who III*, 383.

Not with lamp and fan
but with fire—
beautiful and rollicking—but:
uncontained,
convicted in its violent consumptions;
zealous
and scalding
and unpredictable.

The beautiful, we shine. The hidden smolders, its flames arriving involuntarily, provoked with the sound of the wind, passed gas in the board-rooms of the rich, its heat fixing insides onto faces of others, as it fixed them onto the lepers and the Lazuruses of Rome, so long ago. Their appearance, zombie-esque, evoking frightened disgust, summoning premonitions and paranoias, death's foretaste, acidic belch, nausea; their skin a screen of silver, the taking-place of the horror show: monsters, meannesses, guilty desires, fantastic fears. Freed at last from the captivity.

Illuminating.

Distorting.

The lepers and the Lazaruses.

Looked at, as the prophets would have it.

In the glow

but seldom if ever seen.

So it was with the Worm King who roamed the streets possessed by Soterian fervor, making it certain that the tombs would remain empty for at least another day; saving what others threw away, caring for those left beaten and bloodied as the priests and their sacristans go about their days.

Home was complicated as all homes are. And yet, his public life was Eastertide.

No matter.

The house paint was flaking.

And eccentricities are leprosies, too.

So the neighbors couldn't help it.

They looked at a man who didn't save for rainy days, but who, rather, spent them saving. And all they could see was a monster. A hell erected there on the hill.

And a mirror.

If only they had known what they were seeing.

Lights and mirrors. Fire and insides. We do this to those who are dead, too.

Sometimes we call it a eulogy.

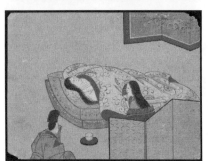

CHAPTER FIVE

Elona's Team

If Natalie did that thing people do when they're asked about their weaknesses at a job interview—that thing when the interviewee tries to spin those weaknesses into strengths—if she were to respond to the question, "What are your growth areas at work?" with the answer of, "I've been told I try too hard and care too much," she wouldn't be lying, in fact she would be too honest. Natalie did care too much, but often it really was a weakness.

Natalie, or Nat as her coworkers called her, due to the fact there was another Natalie on the team when she started, swiped her badge at the side entrance of a nondescript office building. She used the side entrance because the front doors opened into a VA clinic. Most days by 8 a.m. there were anywhere from ten to forty vets outside smoking, a number that would remain or grow throughout the workday. Nat couldn't stand cigarette smoke and couldn't understand why the VA didn't make all the old Vietnam vets quit. She complained about the smoking but nothing was done. Loving Hands of Mercy Hospice, the company she worked for, got a good rate on the offices they had upstairs and weren't about to rock that boat for one of Nat's endless complaints.

Nat climbed the back stairs, down a hallway, and into the offices of Loving Hands of Mercy Hospice. She was greeted by fifteen or so cubicles filled with people on headsets; nobody looked up. Nat walked past the secretaries (who were called team coordinators) and into a large conference room. Nurses in scrubs, a chaplain in clergy gear, social workers in

71

professional outfits, and a team manager (also in scrubs though she hadn't seen a patient in the last decade) populated the space. They were milling about, shooting the breeze and firing up their computers. The group was the Butterfly team, one of five cutely named divisions of the hospice company. The North Side Lemurs were easily the highest performing team, the West Side Wombats' team manager didn't know it but they were currently being investigated for insurance fraud. For a company that dealt in death they sure did enjoy the cute. The Butterfly team was gathering for their weekly interdepartmental team meeting or IDT.

The IDT meeting was basically the same as "rounds" in the hospital. The members of the team, outside of the nurse's aides who were simply too busy for this mandatory meeting, would get together and go through the patients one by one. They would discuss the patient's overall health, wellbeing, medications, existential dread, funeral arrangements, and living conditions, and then vent about what a bunch of entitled pains in the ass the dying were. The meeting was meant to ensure each patient gets the best individual care possible; it didn't always live up to these lofty goals.

After a prayer—Loving Hands of Mercy Hospice and its parent company Fredericks Firearms were very religious outfits—there was a discussion about what to do if an employee gets rear-ended at work. There had been a lot of car accidents as of late. After that conversation and the weekly complaints about too much paperwork and not enough staff, the group jumped into the caseload. This was about an hour after the meeting was set to start. The team was made up of three nurses, two social workers, a chaplain, and a bunch of nurse's aides. The total caseload for the team was sixty-five patients, probably fifteen too many.

Each patient was assigned a nurse case manager. Irene was assigned to the first three that came up in the discussion. Irene was always ready for the meeting, had her notes pulled up on her computer, got to the point, and moved along. Irene had places to be. People appreciated Irene. Nat had the fourth case, people stretched and settled in when the name of the patient was announced, Elona. Nat took five minutes to get her computer to the last note she had written about Elona; after a deep breath, she began her report.

ELONA'S HOUSE

Elona would have called her neighborhood working class. It was the kind of place where you knew your neighbors, because there was only a foot of space between you and them. It was the kind of place Archie Bunker would have to live on his salary, not because he wanted to. Where people of different backgrounds came together because they had no place else. Elona would have called it working class, the people in the neighborhood over would have told their kids not to go there.

Still, Elona's block was pretty nice, as blocks in Elona's neighborhood went. Houses were small and squat but largely kept up. Lawns were mowed. Doors had bars on them, or a security door outside of the front door.

Elona's house was built by her grandfather in the '20s. He bought the kit for the home through the Sears Roebuck Catalogue and did the vast majority of the work himself. Elona had never lived anyplace else. The house was set back from the street, which the neighbors were thankful for. The grass was tall, the gate hung off its hinges, which began giving way during the Clinton administration. The paint on the home was peeled. The paint on the door was scratched to hell by the fifty or so dogs that had called the palace home over the years. The yard was littered with those dogs' leavings, along with a rusted out old swing set more likely to give a child tetanus than a good time. There were beaten and broken children's toys discarded decades earlier and new ones just beginning to molder. The skeleton of what appeared to be the remains of an old Volkswagen Beetle sat in the tall grass. The city had asked them to remove it a number of times, but never bothered following up.

Elona knew the house was in bad shape when she was taken to the hospital a month before. It was far from the first time she had been taken to the hospital. Elona was what was known as a frequent flier. Heart issues, diabetes, obesity, smoking three packs a day, constant falls, and living in filth did a number on her health. The last time she went to the hospital it was due to a cut on her foot. The cut had become infected. Elona didn't even notice the cut at first. She was confined to a wheelchair and rarely put weight on her lower extremities, and as such the cut had festered without her notice. She smelled the wound before she saw that her toes were turning black. Elona lived with her three daughters, six grandkids, and one son-in-law (who was not technically married to Elona's daughter). When Elona called in her middle child to inspect the wound her daughter passed out; her oldest child called the ambulance.

After some time in the hospital, and many attempts by hospital staff to get her to go to a nursing facility, Elona was able to go home. She was in bad shape when she arrived. While in the hospital the doctor discovered what appeared to be a large tumor in Elona's lungs. Elona was too weak for them to biopsy the tumor, which would have involved an invasive procedure that she wouldn't have allowed anyway. This along with some strange labs was enough for the doctors to conclude it was most likely malignant and inoperable even if Elona was healthy enough to go under the knife. Elona had watched her mother and father both face the misery of long, painful, and ultimately futile cancer treatments and wasn't about to put herself through that. The doctor said doing nothing was a death sentence; Elona said that would be fine. She was sent home with hospice care.

Elona's family, like most families, had no real experience with hospice care. They assumed hospice care meant two things: one, that Elona would be dead very soon; and two, they would get around-the-clock support to help them with the endlessly complex and emotionally draining tasks that were required to care for a dying person. The hospice salesperson did nothing to disavow them of this belief. Unfortunately what they believed and what they got were two very different things. What they got was a few nursing visits a week, a nurse's aide, a monthly visit from a social worker, and a chaplain. That along with medications and medical equipment.

The equipment included an oxygen regulator, a bedside commode, and a hospital bed for the commode to sit on the side. Elona had lived upstairs in a little bedroom in the back of the house up until her injury. After being confined to a chair, she usually just slept on the couch in the living room. The hospital bed was going to have to be set up in that same living room, as there was no way to get Elona up to the back bedroom.

The problem was the front room had a lot of stuff in it. There was a TV and a couch; the TV would stay but the couch was going to have to go to make room for the hospital bed. There was a giant china hutch, so massive that it was likely the house would be gone long before anyone moved it, the hutch never actually held fine china. It was filled with the little ceramic elephants and novelty teaspoons Elona had ordered or bought at garage sales throughout the years. Hundreds and hundreds of tiny little elephants in various outfits and colors. The teaspoons were from every state five times over, except Wyoming and the District of Columbia, which she had six and seven spoons for respectively. Once she filled up one fifty-state-plus-DC decorative spoon holder Elona got another. The contents of that hutch were as close to Elona's life's work as anything could be.

The room was littered with the detritus of many childhoods. Some of it should have been removed long ago. Some items, like the stuffed carnival prize bear that had been the dog's enemy before it became his friend and then secret lover, were so common for the family to see lying in the middle of the floor they had simply become part of the decor. There were five stacks of books that reached four feet high on each of the walls, two more stacks, equally tall, of DVDs. There was an old bounce chair that hadn't been used since the youngest had learned to walk three years earlier. There was a plastic play kitchen, the stove's door was ripped off, crayon graffiti covered the side of it.

Besides the toys there was also just garbage. A lot of people lived in the home, and more were in and out. Plastic soda cups, full ashtrays, cans of beer and energy drink littered the room. They cleaned up every so often but Elona's family had largely gotten used to a dirty home and could let a mess go for a while. The day Elona was to arrive home from the hospital the family was given a one-hour window in which to expect the medical supply service to drop off the bed. They were supposed to clean the room before the bed arrived. They did a poor job of it. They may have done a better job but Elona arrived home before her new bed. Meaning she had to sit up in a chair and wait for the bed.

The newly arrived Elona had lost the core strength to sit up in a chair. She could bear slight weight on her foot, enough to pivot, and she was able to sit on the commode long enough to do her business, sometimes. But sitting up for an extended period hurt her back horribly. The family had no choice but to lay her on the bare ground, which brought its own pain. Attending to Elona meant the family simply didn't have the time to get the room properly prepared. They were too busy calling the hospice company, trying to get a little direction and guidance on how to help the woman. When the bed finally did arrive, they only had time to shove everything into one corner of the room and get Elona in the bed. Once she was in bed it was another hour or so to get her comfortable. In the pain and the screaming, the confusion and the fear, they simply didn't get the place picked up. The bulk of the garbage was on the other side of Elona's bed, now hard to get to, hard to see, and mostly forgotten about.

IDT

"I don't know why they don't clean up that front room," Natalie said, beginning the IDT discussion of Elona's case.

"Nat, can you first tell us about the patient and what is going on?" the team manager asked.

"Oh yes. Elona is my seventy-three year old cancer patient." Nat always spoke about patients in the possessive. "She has comorbidities of extreme obesity; she is a very big lady. She also has diabetes, a right foot amputation, and congestive heart failure. Hold on . . ." there was a pause as Nat typed in her computer. "Oh yeah and she has HIV."

"She has HIV as well?" asked the doctor. "Kind of low on the list of comorbidities, isn't it?"

"Yeah, I didn't even notice it before, but I'm looking at my notes and it says HIV." Nat paused for a second. "Doctor, do you think we should make that her primary diagnosis? I don't have any labs for cancer."

"No labs at all for the cancer? Where did we get the diagnosis?"

"The hospital assumed it based on some strange blood work, lethargy, and a possible spot on her lung, but they weren't able to biopsy it."

"Never having seen this patient it's kind of hard to know. It would be nice to have the labs though."

"They aren't gonna send her back to the hospital for the tests."

The doctor paused for a second, "Okay, okay, well maybe we could use HIV or AIDS. Is she showing symptoms?"

"She did have some diarrhea and a mild fever."

"Yes those are symptoms of AIDS I guess we can switch it to that. Let's all remember to be very careful with our Personal Protective Equipment when doing changes on Ms. Elona."

"Well if she has AIDS I'm gonna need some more gloves," Nat spoke up.

"Natalie I just ordered you five boxes of gloves, based on your caseload a box should last a week. You're at triple that," the team manager interjected.

"Sorry but I need the gloves to do the care. You don't want us to get infected out there, do you?"

"No I don't, it's just that corporate set a budget. . . ."

Nat held up a hand as she looked at her computer.

"Oh no, it's Mr. Jones that has HIV not Ms. Elona." Nat made a quick note on her computer, then looked up. "Okay so can I get the gloves or not?"

"You just said the reason you need the gloves doesn't have HIV so no." The team manager was flustered.

"Fine I guess you don't care about us then," Nat mumbled under her breath.

"So, we aren't changing the patient's diagnosis?" the doctor asked.

"You're the doctor, what do you think?" Nat asked.

"Well it depends really," the doctor paused for a second. "HIV or AIDS can be used as a terminal diagnosis, so it's a possibility. But the patient doesn't have AIDS right?"

"Let me just look at my charts." Nat took a second. "No, no she doesn't have AIDS."

"Oh well then I guess we stick with the cancer for now."

"Okay doctor, just to read back. We are not going with the HIV diagnosis, because the patient does not have HIV, correct?" Nat asked. There was a long pause.

"Yes, yes that seems right."

"Okay so I should change it back to the cancer diagnosis?"

"Does he have cancer?"

"She."

"What?"

"She's a she."

"Does she have cancer?"

Nat shrugged her shoulders.

"Hey everyone we have a lot of cases to get to today, can we speed this up?" the team manager asked.

"Yes," the doctor said, looking at her watch.

"Yes, we can speed it up or yes she has cancer?" Nat asked.

"Both, I guess," the doctor replied. "But keep an eye on the HIV."

"Will do. Should I go on with the case?" Nat asked

"Yes," the doctor and the team manager said in unison.

"So first of all this lady is huge, she's huge and her kids either don't want to or have no idea how to take care of her."

ELONA'S

Elona was a big woman; she had been big her entire life. Her parents, who were both poor immigrants, thought of food as love and they loved their little girl a lot. She wasn't happy about being obese. Elona wished she could run around and play with her grandkids. But her knees were bad, she got tired quickly, her back had issues, all of which didn't let her play the way she wanted to. She did love to sit in the living room and watch them play.

When she got back from the hospital, she still got to see them run around the room, only now she couldn't even get out of the bed. The first couple days after she got home Elona could scoot herself to the commode but she got weaker quickly and soon enough getting to the portable john was about as likely for Elona as hopping up and running the Boston Marathon. It sat there, next to the bed, mocking her as she went in the diaper. When this happened Elona tried to keep it to herself, she didn't want to bother the kids, or gross out the grandchildren. Of course, she was in the living room, eventually people were going to smell it and something had to be done about it.

Her daughters tried the best they could. They were nice enough young ladies. They had been in their fair share of trouble now and again. None of them had finished high school, if for nothing else than the people around them never expected them to. They weren't particularly bright or pretty, and never had any money. These keys to an easy life were not handed to them, but they found a way to get by in the world. None of Elona's daughters knew anything about caring for their mom when she got home from the hospital.

The nurse's aide was kind and patient with them. She showed them how to give a bed bath to Elona. How to lift up her skin folds and clean out those damp, dark places where bacteria grew. She showed them how to change sheets without getting Elona out of bed, and how to change her diaper. These tasks are not easy tasks; they were physically demanding and Elona's girls despite being big and strong themselves had their own health issues. Bad backs and knees made it hard to care for their mom. Deeper than that, it wasn't easy to care for Elona because Elona was their mom. All three girls had their issues with the woman. Elona could be an angry person on occasion, she was known to be critical and selfish. She drank sometimes and when she did she was even harder to be around, but she loved her girls and they loved her. Caring for their dying mother, the only parent they had ever had, meant accepting she was dying. They were happy to do the work but that didn't make it any easier. Eventually it got to be too much for the middle daughter, who when she was home retreated to her bedroom.

There was also the fact the girls all had things to do. They were in the prime of their lives. The youngest was working at the Walmart, the middle kid had a no-good boyfriend who demanded much of her time and had little heart for her situation. The oldest had the kids to take care of as well as a job of her own answering phones at the impound lot. The son-in-law-ish ended up doing much of the sitting with Elona, who couldn't be left alone.

At first, neither he nor Elona were comfortable with him doing direct care. It was only when things got really, really bad that he got more hands on.

In the days after she arrived, Elona's pride and her son-in-law's nervousness meant that sometimes Elona would sit in her own waste. Not that it happened often. Eventually even the oldest grandkid would help, though Elona was too big for her to roll on her own. Elona would have to pull herself up on the bed rail so the twelve-year-old could properly clean her grandmother. Elona preferred not to put the little one through this, nor any of her family, so if she could hold it she would wait until the nurse or the aide were on their way to the house. Elona figured it was their job to take care of her, so she might as well get her insurance money's worth. The family largely agreed with this, though the nurse and aide weren't there all that often, which meant the family still did the vast majority of the care.

IDT

"She is dirty every time I get there, and the aide says the same thing. Her skin is going to start breaking down and I don't think the family cares at all." Nat sounded worried. "Last time the poop was all dry. It took me like an hour to get her cleaned up. The son-in-law just stood there watching me; he didn't even help. Elona's a big woman, it's hard on my back. The least he could do would have been to lend a hand. I try to educate him but he just doesn't seem to listen no matter how long I talk with him. In fact every time I'm in that house I spend at least an hour there. I try to tell them I have more patients to get to but it's in one ear and out the other."

ELONA'S

"Is that nurse coming again today?" Elona called out to her son-in-law.

"Tomorrow I think," he replied.

"Oh thank God, that lady was here for like half an hour last time. I wish she would just hurry it up. She takes so long to get me cleaned up."

"I know I saw her last time. I wanted to help her out, she is so particular I thought I'd get yelled at. Didn't want to mess her up."

"Yeah she's the professional, and she sure lets you know it. You'd probably just slow her down, and with all those other patients she is so busy taking care of, probably best just to let her do her job. Still you are quicker and I think you actually get me cleaner."

"I'll tell you that aide is a good teacher. She showed me all the tricks. The nurse keeps telling me stuff but I have no idea what she is talking about. She's always going on about Kennedy ulcers and what is it, cock sists."

"I think it's coccyx."

"Yeah whatever, I work on cars, I don't know anything about oxygen levels or impacted stool. She looks at me like I'm an idiot every time she tries to tell me what to do. I'd like to see her fix a flat tire."

"Now, now she drives me nuts too but we need her and I need the medicine. I think she is trying her best to help."

"Yeah, you're right I know. She's doing a good job too. I just get a little frustrated with all these people coming in and out of the house. It's like we are running a hospital out of here, which is fine, it's just we got stuff to do." The son-in-law felt bad as soon as he said it. He didn't want Elona to feel any more like a burden than she already did.

"I know, I know, and I'm sorry I brought them in here."

"Oh you don't have to be sorry Elona; you need the help. I'm sorry, I just get frustrated."

"Hey, my dear son-in-law, I don't know what we'd do without you either. You know when she brought you home I wasn't sure about you."

"Was it the tattoos?" he said with a smile.

"No, I'm just not used to my daughter dating a guy that could out-party me. You're such a lightweight. That said, I want you to know, before this all goes wrong, how happy I am to have you around." The son-in-law was taken aback, he wasn't used to his normally hard-nosed mother-in-law talking so sweet. A real tear drop squeezed out over the one tattooed just below his eye.

"Oh Ma, don't talk that bullshit, everything is gonna be fine." There was a pause.

"Yeah, you're right it will," Elona said to nobody in particular.

IDT

"Does that son-in-law give anybody else a bad vibe?" Nat asked, nobody answered, she was undeterred. "I mean I don't want to judge but he has all those tattoos on his neck. I'm not saying that makes him a bad person, it's just, I don't know I get a little nervous when I'm there."

"Do you need security to go with you?" the team manager asked.

"I don't know, maybe. It's not that he's ever done anything threatening or something like that. It's just how he kind of sits there and watches me work. It's just a little, oh I don't know, strange I guess. That's the word for it. It just makes me feel unsafe." "Unsafe" was a word the team manager was trained to pay special attention to.

"Well, like I said, if you really feel unsafe you should have our security team go with you."

"Okay I've never used the security before, so do you set that up?"

"What happens is you make a request. You just go online and fill out an application saying what you need the security for. Once they approve it, you can call them to set up the visit time. I think they need a three-day window. You will have to find a time that works for all of you. It might mean you have to change your regular visit time. They'll meet at the house and wait outside during your visit."

"They won't even come in?"

"Well, it might be uncomfortable for the family if you have some big off-duty cop just standing in the corner of the room while you work."

"Will they work around my schedule?"

"They have their own work, but I think they do the best they can."

"So, I might have to change my whole day around to go with them?"

"Yeah maybe. They seem to prefer the morning and the end of the day best, but hopefully you will be able to work all that out with them."

"Are you sure the team scheduler can't set this up for me?"

"No, it's your schedule Nat, you have to manage it."

"You know what, I think it's okay. I'm not gonna reach out to them. If it gets worse maybe, but I think I'll be fine." Nat tried to sound confident.

"Are you sure? We don't want you to feel unsafe." The manager did not seem to be surprised by Nat's sudden change of position.

"Well you make a good point, I don't want the family to feel uncomfortable."

"But the security will be outside."

"I know, but what if they could see them out the window? I'll keep it in mind for another time."

"Okay, but your safety is our main concern."

"It's fine. I'm not really worried right now as everything is kind of status quo over there. The patient is alert and oriented currently, but I am worried about what will happen when she starts to decline."

"Do you think they might call 911?" The team manager sounded concerned. A hospice family calling 911 did not look good to management.

"I tried to educate the son-in-law not to. I told him to call us first if the patient stops breathing, but I don't know if he really understood me."

"If they are going to call 911, we have to ask if these people should really be on hospice. I mean if they want the patient to live so badly maybe they should be seeking aggressive treatment?" The doctor sounded reasonable as she chimed in.

"That's what I was thinking," Nat said, trying to hide her excitement at the prospect of dropping Elona as a patient. One less case in an already over full caseload.

"Why don't we give it a few more weeks and reevaluate," the team manager replied, not wanting to lose a case and look bad to her superiors.

ELONA'S

"Since we are on the subject, what do you want me to do if you stop breathing or have a heart attack or something? Because that nurse sure had a lot of ideas on the subject. If I'm here I'll do whatever you want me to do, just let me know."

"Like what do you mean, if my heart stops? What choices do I have?"

"Well the nurse thinks it's best if we don't do anything. She says we should call the hospice and then they can come out and pronounce you dead." The son-in-law was a pretty straightforward matter-of-fact guy but even he almost choked on the word "dead."

"Do nothing, just leave me dead. I don't know, it seems like we should do something, right?" Elona almost giggled as she said it. "I mean shouldn't they try to bring me back or whatever? The paddles and mouth to mouth and all that. What do you think?" The son-in-law threw his hands up and took a step back.

"Don't ask me Ma, you tell me what you want. It's your life. I don't have a clue."

"Well I don't know that I don't want anything done. I mean should they at least try to bring me back? I'm not saying they need to airlift me to the hospital, but it seems to me you don't just let a person die, right? Can't they do something?"

"It seems like they can. I mean they have those electric zapper things all over town. I saw one in the grocery store yesterday. They gotta work, right? If they didn't they wouldn't have them everywhere, right?"

"You'd think. . . . Yea they must. I think . . . um . . . yeah they should try to save me. I don't want to just give up, right? Sure, if that time comes, if you find me not breathing I think you should have them do whatever it is they can to save me."

"Okay, but who's gonna tell the nurse? She's not gonna like it." Both looked nervous.

ELONA'S

Two Weeks Later

Elona no longer spoke, she no longer moved, she no longer sang, or shouted, or argued, or gave up, or fought. She no longer did much of anything. She lay in the bed and stared at the ceiling, maybe through it. Who could tell? She still had needs, toileting and cleaning. She stopped eating but some animal instinct in her would still lead her to suck on a sponge dipped in water if someone put it in her mouth, though it made her cough.

The family was around all the time, except for the middle daughter. She tried to be in the room when she could but found it too painful to watch her mother slowly die. Elona's weight meant she could last a long time without food, though her face had thinned out and some of those reserves were already drained.

Elona's oldest daughter was worried about her mom not eating. Elona didn't moan or whine, but she appeared uncomfortable and her daughter worried that her mom was starving. Her daughter, like Elona herself, had grown up thinking that food was love. Elona was the type of mom to cook a meal and order sides from three different places depending on how crispy their mozzarella sticks were and if the wings had the right amount of meat on them. Elona loved to eat and so did the kids. Watching her lie there, not eating anything, it broke her daughter's heart.

It broke her heart so much that when nobody was looking Elona's oldest child would sneak her mom food. Not giant steaks or anything. She wasn't force feeding her mom burgers and ribs. Spoonfuls of ice cream, little bits of chocolate and milkshakes. Things she knew her mom liked and that she thought would be easy for her to swallow. Sometimes it worked, but other times Elona would cough and sputter, like she was choking. One day after a five-milliliter slurp of half melted ice cream Elona was hacking like crazy when the son-in-law walked in the room.

"Did you give her something to eat?" he asked, looking at his sister-in-law with concern.

"Only a little bite," she replied.

"Remember what the nurse said, we don't want your mom to ass-perspire, aspire, ass-kate."

"I think it was aspirate," the daughter said.

"Yeah that, she said it could make your mom really sick." The son-in-law pointed to the cancer-riddled body three-quarters comatose on the bed. "Or sicker, I guess."

IDT

"She is choking her mother," Nat said to the group at the next IDT meeting. The boss had asked that everybody move quickly through their patients at this meeting as there was new information about the 401k and an upgrade in the electronic medical record she needed to walk them through after the patients were discussed. Every two months there was an upgrade in the medical record that for a week would cause the entire team's computers to act up, and at the end of the week after thousands of complaints the electronic medical record company would reverse the changes they made. Each time this happened an hour or two of the meeting would be dedicated to disgruntled conversation about the change and a nostalgia for the "old days" of paper charting. Those same people forgot all the complaining they did about the paper charting in the old days.

The team manager was hoping Nat would kind of shuffle through her patients like the other nurses. Say that everything was status quo and the care plan was effective. Depending on how deep Nat wanted to dive the meeting could be an hour, or it could be three. Nat had nowhere special to be.

"I keep telling them she is aspirating on her food and that daughter just keeps feeding her. She is going to kill her own mother. Elona is going to get pneumonia and die."

"Have you educated them about the dangers of feeding a dying person?"

"They don't listen to me, they think not feeding somebody is the same as killing them. It's like they don't care about their mother at all. They just keep feeding her whenever I'm not around. I told them she was too sick to eat, that her body had lost the ability to swallow or even do anything with the food once it did get into the stomach. This is what I said. I said to the daughter, 'Elona is so very, very sick that if you feed her at all she might die.'" Nat looked at the social worker. "You were there, I told her that right before you asked which funeral home they were gonna use." The social worker nodded in agreement.

"It's just so hard to get it through some of these families' heads that we aren't starving the patients, we just aren't feeding them. That withholding food isn't withholding love; it is love. I just don't understand why they have such a hard time with the concept." The rest of the group either agreed or were too bored to comment on the subject. The chaplain was regularly checking his watch.

"And I'm still very worried about what the family is going to do when she stops breathing. I think they are going to call 911. I keep telling the son in law that CPR is going to break Elona's ribs and she is going to end up on a ventilator in the hospital. Even if they can bring her back it will cause nothing but pain and hurt. She will never be the same again."

"Just so that I have it right in my notes, the patient is no longer speaking or eating or aware of her surroundings, correct?" the doctor asked.

"Yes doctor, that's true," Nat said quickly to the doctor and then turned back to the group. "I told him that she would be a mess if they were to bring her back, but he kept telling me she insisted that 'something be done' if her heart stops."

"Well keep on educating, our team got a big ding from corporate last month when we had, what was it, five patients get sent to the hospital before they died. Looked bad on the hospital's death records and looked bad on us. If we keep sending patients to the hospital to die we aren't going to get any more referrals. Let's try and make sure that this family doesn't call 911 if the patient stops breathing." Nat sighed.

"Okay, I'll try, but these people just love to call the ambulance. I know I said this before but I'm not sure this patient is hospice appropriate."

"Do you believe this could be more of a spiritual issue than a medical one?" the doctor asked. Whenever the doctor didn't like how a family was behaving, and "education" had failed, the doctor would then dive into the spiritual side of things. "Is the chaplain on the case?"

"I am," the chaplain replied.

"Can you get them to just let the patient die?" There was a long pause.

"Um, well I'm not really sure that's my job. We have discussed the issue but the patient has made it very clear that she wants 'something to be done' if her heart stops and the family is uncomfortable not granting her wishes."

"I know but it's just the wrong choice she made. They are Catholic, right?" the doctor asked, for some reason the patient's religion was printed, along with age, illness, and address, on the brief fact sheet passed out at the start of every meeting.

"The patient and the family are Catholic historically, but nobody has been involved with the church or the faith for years."

"Still they are Catholic, can't you tell them it's okay with the church to let people die naturally?" The doctor, who was not religious, had learned this fact someplace and never failed to bring it up whenever she felt spirituality could solve a problem.

"I'm not sure that's really how faith works," the chaplain responded nervously. Doctors are not used to being challenged. If the doctor says something, the team is supposed to accept it. If the doctor gave them lotto numbers it was the team's job to go out and buy the tickets, and when they lost they blamed it on the person doing the drawing not the doctor. It was lucky for the chaplain Nat chimed in.

"Oh doctor, I don't think the family is gonna listen to the chaplain, or a priest, or even God Almighty. The family is gonna do what they want to do. Also there is another issue, the family wants a refill on the morphine."

"How long has it been since their last refill?" the doctor asked.

"That's the thing, doctor. They've never wanted a refill before. They wouldn't even touch the stuff. I had asked them over and over again to give it to the patient when she was getting angry or uncomfortable, when she couldn't sleep or before they or we were going to provide care. They wouldn't do it at all. Even when the patient was pounding on her chest in pain, they were still very resistant to giving the medications. I practically had to beg them to give her Tylenol."

"Why do you think that is?" the doctor asked.

"We get all these patients that think giving someone morphine is going to either kill them or make them addicted. That must have been what they thought. Last week I spoke with the daughter for over an hour about it."

ELONA'S

Last Week

Nat was going through the bottles of medicine. Checking to see how much was being used, what might need a refill, what could be removed from the medication list, what was too expensive for the hospice to keep paying for, or if any were about to expire. Natalie picked up the tiny bottle of concentrated morphine. A little bottle with enough of the drug to stop a buffalo or Keith Richards in their tracks. The bottle was full and the seal on it had not been broken.

"You'll still haven't used the morphine at all have you? Don't you think it would be better if she was comfortable all the time?" Nat asked the daughter.

"My mother always told me that she would rather be awake and know what was going on around her than to be knocked out on medications."

"Even if she was in pain?"

"She doesn't look like she's in pain to me." Elona was laying peacefully in the bed. The only motion she made at all was to gently tap her hand on her chest. The rhythmic motion was about all Elona had done since she stopped talking.

"You don't see that with her hand?"

"What?"

"Her hand, she is hitting her chest." Nat pointed at Elona's hand, which was moving even slower and more gently now that they were both paying attention to it.

"You think that means she's in pain?"

"Oh, definitely."

"How do you know?"

"I've been doing this a long time honey." Nat was the same age as the daughter and had been working in hospice for eighteen months. "I've seen it all before and that is pain."

"Has anyone woken up and told you they were in pain when they did something like that?" The son-in-law chimed in; he was more interested than anything else.

"Sir, please don't argue with me. I'm the professional here and I'm just trying to help all of you." Nat turned back toward the daughter. "In my professional opinion the patient is in pain, and we should be medicating people who are in pain. There is no reason to leave a person in pain if we can fix it. It is a problem we can solve."

"But she said she would rather be in pain than be doped up."

"Yes, people say that but it's not true, they just don't understand what they are saying."

"So, you're saying even if she doesn't want it we should give her the morphine."

"No, what I'm saying is that she doesn't know what she wants. We are to medicate people in pain, that is our job, so I think you should give her the drugs. At least if you want to give your mother the very best care possible. I'm saying that my patient needs to be medicated." There was a pause as the daughter thought about it.

"Well, I guess you are the nurse and you know best. Sure, okay, let's give her the medication." With a shaky hand the daughter cracked open the bottle and put a couple of drops under her mother's tongue.

"Okay, well done now just look and see how the pain goes away." The patient was still touching her chest. "Looking better already." The daughter, if she was honest with herself, would admit she couldn't see any difference, but she had just given her mother drugs against her explicit wishes so . . . "You know, you're right, she does look better."

IDT

"Since they started giving the stuff they have been going through those meds like crazy, and, at the same time, time Elona's sister has gotten involved. I don't want to say it but I can't help but wonder if she might be diverting some of the medication."

"You think that the sister might be taking the medicine?" The team manager, who moments before had appeared on the verge of sleep, was all of a sudden very interested. There had recently been a segment on *Newsline* about hospice and home health medications being stolen and either taken or sold on the streets, and the executive suite folks were making it their mission in life that it stop.

"Well here's the thing, you know me, I don't like to judge at all. But this woman is strange. The other day I go over there. She opens the door, doesn't say a word to me, just walks over to the couch in the corner and passes out. She didn't even seem to mind the bugs in the corner."

"Bugs?"

"Yeah we'll get to that, there is a real bug problem at that house. But, this sister just passes out on the couch, doesn't say a word to me. She has all the shades drawn so the room is pitch black. Her hair is a mess, she has all these dirty, I don't know, like prison tattoos all over her. Like, I don't want to judge but she gets there and all of a sudden they need more medication every couple of days. It seems suspect to me."

"Well, what do you want to do about it Nat? Do we need to make a complaint to the Department on Aging?" the team manager asked.

"Oh I don't think so, I really am not sure about the medication being diverted, and making those reports is a huge hassle."

"We can put them on a medication count. Make them keep a detailed log. That way we know exactly when and why they are giving the medications to the patient."

"That could work," Nat replied.

"Okay, can you go over there today and tell them about the log?"

"Oh today, well I have a lot going on today. I'm not sure if I'll have time to get over there."

"Okay well I can get the travel nurse to cover a patient or two of yours if that would help."

"I don't think any of my clients are going to want a travel nurse."

"Well, I get that but sometimes we don't have a choice. If you really think the medications are being diverted it has to be addressed. When is your next visit?" Nat flipped a few pages on the computer screen to find her calendar. "I'm set to go tomorrow."

"Do you think it can wait until then?"

"Yeah I think it can. It's not like they are asking for the medication every two seconds, it's just they didn't use any for weeks and now they need refills. Who is going to tell them about the log?"

"You are going to have to tell them," the team manager responded.

"Why should I tell them that I need them to fill out the log?"

"Same reason you told me, that the medication is going a little too fast and we need to look into why."

"What if they get mad at me? Can't you call them? I need to keep up a good relationship with them."

"No Nat I can't be calling your patients all the time. You're the one who has seen the possible diversion, not me. You'll have to let them know."

"Well then why don't we just wait on it. If they ask for a few more refills, I'll have them do the log."

"No Nat, you said this woman was exhibiting strange behavior. I need you to address it now. This is a big thing at the corporate level. Linda, our CFO's daughter, recently went to rehab for a marijuana addiction and she is very sensitive to the subject. You are gonna have to take care of this." There was a long pause.

"Maybe I should make the report to the Department on Aging," Nat said almost to herself, but then thought about the endless paperwork and time sitting on hold involved. "Well I guess if Linda says so." Nat took another long pause. "It might mess up all the good will I've built with this family, but if I have to, I have to."

ELONA'S

Two Days Later

Elona's son-in-law shut the door behind Nat. He waved as she walked to the gate past the rusted-out car and kids' toys. She stepped over a pile of dog poop that nobody had cleaned up, shaking her head as she did. Nat did not look back to see the wave. The son-in-law turned into the house where Elona was sleeping, or in a coma, on the bed, and Elona's sister Kim was sitting on the couch, a shocked expression on her face.

"Did that nurse just accuse me of being a heroin addict?"

"I think she did," the son-in-law responded.

"Did she just threaten to call the cops on me for doing exactly what she trained us to do? I mean you didn't even want to give the morphine at first, right?"

"She told us we were bad people for not giving it. She practically demanded we give the medicine."

"I left my family and my job to come here and help out. My daughter has to pay a babysitter to watch my new baby grandson so I can be here, and she threatens to call the cops on me for giving my sister pain medicine; medicine that she demanded we give."

"I never liked that nurse," the son-in-law responded.

"She says I was acting strange because I didn't talk to her and fell asleep the other day. This was strange behavior. I didn't talk to you," Kimbal said to an invisible person, "because you were two hours late and I wasn't able to get a nap. I didn't talk to you because I was up all damn night worrying that my sister was dead next to me. I didn't talk to you because I had never been so tired in all my life. I needed sleep and figured if my sister was with the professional, the person whose job it is to take care of her, I could grab a couple of minutes. If that's strange behavior I don't know what normal behavior could possibly be. You tell me, are we supposed to sweep and mop before she gets here? Brew her a pot of tea and set it out with cookies for her every time she is going to visit? We aren't supposed to take care of her, are we? Isn't she supposed to take care of us?"

"I never liked that lady," the son-in-law responded. "Always so judgmental, but we need her. Without her we have no medication, no bed, no diapers or wipes. Without the nurse we don't have the aide or the social worker. We need the help so I guess we just have to put up with her. Let me see that log." Kimbal handed the son-in-law a sheet of paper provided by Nat. It has on it a time for when the morphine was given, how much, and the response. "So when are we supposed to give the medicine now?"

"The nurse said only to give it when Elona says she's in pain."

"But Elona doesn't talk anymore," Kimbal sounded exacerbated.

"She also said we could give the medication if Elona looks like she is in pain."

"How do we know that?"

"I have no idea." The two stared at Elona for a moment who was looking up at the ceiling reaching her hand out toward something that only she could see.

"Is that a sign of pain?"

"I think she said it was a sign of agitation."

"What's the difference?"

"I don't know."

"Neither do I."

"She also said we should medicate if there is the possibility she might be in pain."

The son-in-law looked confused. "How do we know when she might be in pain?

"The nurse said to give her the medication before we change her, or wash her, or do any real care for her."

"I change her every two hours. She can't mean I'm supposed to give her medication every two hours, can she?"

"Well we are only giving it every four hours now and that was enough that we were accused of doing the drugs ourselves. So to answer your question, I don't know." Kimbal threw up her hands.

"Okay, where is that 800 number? I think we need to call the hospice and get someone to make sense of this stuff." The son-in-law walked off muttering under his breath, "I can't stand that nurse."

IDT

One Week Later

Elona was second on the list of patients that had died over the previous week. At the start of the IDT meeting the bereavement coordinator would read the names and ask for comments on the patients that had died. The staff, mostly the nursing staff, would then provide insight as to what the "bereavement risk" for the surviving families was. Nobody, including the bereavement coordinator, had any idea what the word "risk" meant in this context. Still, families would be categorized into low, medium, and high risk categories. Each category was unique to the given nurse reporting off. While some nurses listed nearly every family as "low," Nat tended to see more issues.

"Oh, Elona's family is definitely a high, higher than high risk maybe, for bereavement," Nat spoke with conviction. The bereavement coordinator, being used to Nat's nature, was taciturn in response.

"And why would it be high, Natalie?"

"Well first of all, the last couple of days the family just did not stop calling the office. Every little thing that was happening they kept reaching out. There was just no way to deal with them."

"Was there some kind of crisis at the end of life?" the bereavement coordinator asked.

"No, nothing out of the ordinary. The patient did get some apnea and had some terminal restlessness, but I mean that happens at a lot of deaths. They just couldn't seem to work it out."

"How were they after the death?"

"Oh they lost it. They called 911 though I had told them over and over again to call us and not the ambulance. Luckily the son-in-law had the presence of mind to call us second, and a good thing the family decided to sign the do not resuscitate order the day before. I want to thank the social worker for helping with that, I don't know how you got it done. I couldn't get them to sign one to save my life."

"They called me and asked, I didn't do anything really besides bring the form out to them," the social worker replied humbly.

"Whatever you did I'm glad you did because if you hadn't they would have taken her to the hospital," the team manager interjected.

"So how was the family coping emotionally?" The bereavement coordinator tried to recenter the conversation.

"Like I said they lost it, I thought the medics were gonna have to take one of the daughters to the hospital. She was screaming and crying; I thought she was going to hyperventilate. The patient's sister was crying, and seemed angry. Not that she would talk to me. The son-in-law was holding up okay, but I would worry about him in the long run. That guy has some anger issues, and let's not forget about the drug diversion."

"Did we prove that?"

"Not really but still the guy just seemed off to me, the sister too," the team collectively rolled their eyes, everyone seemed "off" to Nat. She didn't notice the eye roll, no matter how often it happened.

"Hey Nat, do you know when they are going to pick up the hospital bed from the house?" the social worker chimed in.

"No I don't, why?"

"The son-in-law called me early this morning saying the bed was still in the living room and they would like to get the room cleaned up."

"Huh, they didn't seem to be worried about getting it cleaned up when Elona was alive. But no, I have no idea when they are going to pick up the equipment."

"Did you call the service company to come and get it?" the team manager asked.

"Wait, I'm supposed to do that now? I'm confused, I thought the secretary was the one that called the company." Nat sounded more angry than confused.

"If an RN attends a death it is their responsibility to make sure to call the equipment service and let them know when the family can be there to pick it up. We went over this in our staff meeting last month."

"I didn't hear that. You know this company keeps putting more and more on the shoulders of the nurses. . . ." Nat and the team manager spent the next twenty-five minutes arguing about whose task is what and who should take care of what when. Elona's name did not come up again. The bereavement coordinator wrote "low" risk in her notes and called the house two weeks later to check in on the family.

ELONA'S

Two Weeks Later

The house phone rang; it never rang and if it did it was always some sales person or a political campaign. The son-in-law had only just found out, when the overdue notice came, that Elona had been paying the phone bill all these years and now that she was gone the phone company wanted their due from someone else. He had been opening a lot of mail like that. It hurt him to read the letters, not because of the money but because each one confirmed just how much Elona had done for him and his family.

Normally he would have let the phone ring but the son-in-law was bored. Up until a few weeks before his life had been filled with the heart-breaking, back-breaking, and surprisingly meaningful task of caring for Elona. Without that task, and with his regular job not calling him back after his leave of absence to care for Elona, the son-in-law had nothing to do. He was bored and sick of staring at the hospital bed where Elona had died, and which nobody had come to pick up. He thought of taking it out to the garage but he was worried he might break it and the family would be stuck with the bill. For a distraction, if nothing else, he picked up the phone.

"Hello?" the son-in-law tried to convey through his voice how little he wanted to be talking to whoever was on the other end.

"Hi," a voice trying to sound both somber and kind at the same time said back. "I'm the bereavement coordinator with the hospice and I was just calling to reach out and check in to see how the family is holding up."

"Oh," the son-in-law thought for a moment. The tone in his voice changed as he answered her question. "I guess we're alright. I mean we miss her and all but Elona was pretty sick for a while. It took us, really me, a long time to see just how sick she was. It got pretty bad near the end."

"How so?"

"First she had those big gaps in her breath. It was like she was drowning or something. My wife couldn't stand to watch her mother gasping for air like that. It was even worse for Elona's middle daughter. She really wanted to see her mom, but every time she came into the room the poor kid would just break down. You might need to talk with her. She's having a real hard time."

"Sure, sure you can give her my number."

"I will, it wasn't just the breathing, though I've never seen anything like that."

"Yeah that end of life apnea can be hard to watch."

"It was . . . well also . . . um she kept pulling at her clothes. For the last day and half she didn't stop moving. The woman hadn't moved except to tap on her chest. I don't know why she did that, but those last few days she kept on clawing at her clothing. We had to be careful with the medication because the nurse thought we were stealing it. Maybe if we gave her more it could have helped her be calm at the end. I don't know. Elona's sister was so angry about that. It took everything for her not to cuss that nurse out when she came."

"I'm sorry to hear you didn't like your nurse."

"I guess some people just don't get along. She did seem to know her stuff though. In all honesty she did help us a lot, just the medication stuff got confusing is all. The social worker, she was great. She really explained the do not resuscitate thing. It made a lot of sense once Elona got as sick as she did. I'm glad they didn't do CPR on her. I thought they would when my wife messed up and called 911. She didn't mean to, it was more of instinct. You know you see someone die, you call 911. That's the way it's supposed to be, right? She was worried we could get in trouble with the cops if we didn't report the death. One of her friends at work's cousin got locked up for something like that, at least that's the story they told. But the medics were cool; they didn't do nothing to her once they got a look at that form."

"Well I'm glad to hear that worked out."

"It did, but I guess we are doing fine now. Kind of a relief actually, it was just too much to see her like that. She was . . ." the son-in-law got a little choked up, "she was a great woman. She treated me like her own son. Nobody ever did that for me before. We're gonna miss her but we're here for each other. I think we'll be fine."

"Having support can make all the difference. Is there anything else you need from us?" the son-in-law almost said no, but then spoke up.

"Well yes, actually, can you have someone come and get this damn hospital bed out of here? We want our living room back. Haven't been able to properly clean this house since they brought the thing in here."

"Nobody has come to pick up the bed?"

"No."

"I'm so sorry, let me call the office and see what I can do." After a few pleasantries and goodbyes the bereavement coordinator hung up. She called the office and two hours later someone came to get the bed, and with it the last trace of Elona's final days. There was relief and sadness in the house.

Interlude

Dissolution's Revelation

From the time it is foretold, until its end, each person involved in its life already knows the terrible truth: the fullness of the beauty of bread is never perfectly known until it arrives at the agony of its final hour. It is only then that, being eaten, it dies, giving up its ghost for the life and joy of others.

For this reason, the ancient messianics declared that, among all of the available elements, their godhuman (whom they called *the Bread*) picked bread as its sign—a tool to point human bodies toward the heavens. For it was there, they believed, that the Bread sat. Mystical and majestic. Its forehead casting beams of light from cushions made of right hands.

The sect also understood that this sign was not a sign alone.

Their communities celebrated the advent of spring with a solemn period dedicated entirely to death. Songs of praise were omitted from worship, replaced with absence or by the sounds of a dirge. Dust was traced onto skin. Garments were torn. And the whole thing concluded with a recitation of the very last words muttered by the Bread on its very last day.

The season itself was prefaced with a story. The Bread ascends a mountain. Arriving at the trail's end, it is greeted by a cloud who, in reverence, bows down, becoming fog in its humble descent. Lifting its eyes, the cloud is met with a surprise. There, with the Bread, two figures have appeared: the Order Maker and the Agitator of Kings! Ancient men, faces afire, their bodies are left unconsumed, embracing, and overjoyed. A holy convocation. A meeting of faith, space, and time.

Quickly, however, it is revealed that what they had received as intimate joy has, in actuality, been subjected to another's gaze. The Bread has been followed, its students, voyeurs, in a tizzy, emerging from the weeds.

The earth shakes, as well. Not from fear. But in rhythm with a thunderclap. Arriving as a thief. Breaking windows. Fracturing skies. As the heavens, exposed, are forced to testify. *This Bread is Love. This Bread is loved. And this Bread, beloved, is sacred, indeed.*

At this proclamation, the fog ascends, taking the ancients and the voice with it. The Bread, left alone, sets its face toward the city about which the oracles had foretold.

Here, the reading ends, setting the tone for the weeks to follow, not to be picked up again until the end of the season when at last devotees will find the Bread in that city. Arrested and abused by those who fear leaven, the Bread will be hung high upon a hilltop, no one hiding in the weeds, exposed on purpose, for the whole world to see. It is only then, in the nausea of devastation and in the Bread now broken, that the Bread's students and friends will finally come to realize who the Bread really was.

Michaelangelo once imagined *man*, naked and pale, his finger flaccidly drooping toward the Divine—yet, nonetheless approached in its impotence by the outstretched finger of God. After the Bread was gone and the community still remained, this is what began to happen to the bread that they were baking. In its gesturing, their bread was greeted. Not by a nearness producing a gap, one finger not quite touching another. But by a full embrace. An adoration. A cloud bowing down. A fog.

The bread pointed and the Bread pointed back. With a hug. A touch so powerful that it left the bread transformed. Not only in posture or figure. But to the core. So that, there, pointing and embraced, the bread became the Bread itself. Broken, shared, tasted, and seen.

Bread is a sign that is more than a sign. It points. As it points, that toward which it points draws near—so near, that the bread is touched. Touched, it is transformed, becoming the presence of that very thing toward which it had been pointing in the first place. Sharing a meal, recipients of the bread perceive the Bread that is presenced in the bread. This is fleeting as, again, it takes place only at the moment of dissolution. Such is the life of a sacrament. It's here. And then it's gone.

There is another sacrament. One that no sect has yet acknowledged. Neither in declarations nor in catechetical instruction. This is not because the sects don't believe in it—they do—but because their traditions and their hierarchies, for millennia, have preached disdain for the vessel in which it is contained: breath and blood and dry cracked clay.

It was not always this way. The lives of the messianics were once marked by bodies invigorated, revived through spiritual acts of ecstasy, eyes euphoric, backward rolling, joy remaining for days. Wind, spirit, love: these their bodies welcomed in as breath, as smoke, as fire, moaning expulsions, nonsensical cries. Codswallop. Gibberish. Laughter. Glossolalia.

They shared in communistic feasts where each would eat each one's fill, taking leftovers home for family and for occasional late night snacks. Pleasure and longing took their place at the center of the community. For decades. Here, the body, healthy and well-fed, was celebrated, alive, and unbound.

Then a new generation of leaders arrived. And quickly all of that was buried. The body, they condemned, calling it unkind names. *Concupiscent. Cage. The Cause of All That is Wrong!* From it, they claimed, no good could arrive.

If a member causes you to sin, cut it off! Cut it off!
If it tempts or if it tests you in any way, throw it away, throw it away!
Toss it, toss it, to the fire, to the flames!
Toss it, toss it, toss it away.

These were the words of their anthem, sung while swinging machetes. Chopping. Hacking. Scraping. Until the job was done. They swallowed every cord. They left no trace. They made certain no memory would remain. The marriage, nullified. The kid? Cut in half. Body and soul were forever estranged.

Severed from spirit and mind, the body was quickly and easily reduced into a caricature, a cartoon, a sketch—unseen even as it was viewed—subjected to the ignorant, arrogant, and reductive gaze of the ones called theologians. And yet, all the while, the sacrament within it remained. Intact. Buried. But alive.

And so we wonder. What is this Sacrament? Of what is it composed? What is its name? What does it do? How, in us, does it feel? These questions we will explore briefly below.

WHAT IS THIS SACRAMENT? OF WHAT IS IT COMPOSED?

Unlike the Sacrament of Bread that is made and can be touched by human hands, this sacrament simply exists and is only touched from inside of our skin. Like the Bread of the Table, this sacrament is composed of at least two elements, each with its own instincts and personality. Distinct though they are, however, they are also connected. To borrow a theological metaphor, each is a pole that inhabits a sphere.[1] Though, from the surface of one pole, the other may seem foreboding and alien; from a distance, we are able to see that they're conjoined at the core. They grow from the same earth. They are shaped by the same movements of the same ocean waves.

WHAT IS ITS NAME?

This sphere, in its wholeness, is the sacrament that we now know as the Sacrament of Expectation (or sometimes the Anticipatory Sacrament—the names are used interchangeably). The names of the poles, as you may have guessed, are Anxiety and Hope.

WHAT DOES IT DO?

As noted above, sacraments are signs that point. The Sacrament of Expectation points in at least two ways.

First, the pointing of this sacrament is both future-oriented and emotional. It is felt as a premonition, a hunch, a prayer, a suspicion, an intuition. It is a funny feeling, a *what if?*, a what about, and so on. It is a feeling of feeling-already that which has not yet taken place. It's a feeling of feeling already that which the sacrament is gesturing toward. Known among many as a *forestate*, it's a feeling that, feeling already, invites the body, in one way or another, to salivate or simply to prepare. Said differently, feeling already that toward which it points, the Sacrament of Expectation gestures toward *a future*—or, rather, *futures*: happenings or events that, for now, exist only in potentiality. Lying in wait. It is this multiplicity of futures, commingling in potentiality that complicates this sacrament's pointing. Also, it is what

---

1. Tillich, *Dynamics of Faith*, 47.

makes its pointing unique. This uniqueness of pointing is also the source of this sacrament's second differentiating quality.

Second, unlike other sacraments, this sacrament does not point in one direction, alone. As futures and fate are many and unfixed, the Sacrament of Expectation is unable to fixate. Unlike the bread who only and ever points toward the Bread, and unlike the water who points only toward its Bird (a topic we have not covered here, but which I invite you to investigate), the pointing of this sacrament is multidirectional and a bit more scrambled. This multidirectionality is the source of the sacrament's considerable emotional impact upon the human body.

HOW, IN US, DOES THIS SACRAMENT FEEL?

As the pointing of the Sacrament of Expectation is less of a pointing and more of a pirouette, it often produces a dizzied sensation. As the body partakes of this dizziness, the elements themselves can begin to drift. Hope and anxiety melt. And they merge. And as they mix, they become much more complex. Hybrid emotions are born, swimming and unpredictable. Just as a great pianist can play three melodies at once, so the body sings in endless emotional symphony. No field of study has produced an adequate name for this state. It is usually described simply as *mixed emotions*. Other times it is called a state of erosion or overwhelm. Whatever we call it, it is sacred and sacramental.

In these state(s), there emerges in the body an unspoken imperative: *With heart, hands, and hair, stand on edge! At attention. Lamps lit and ready. Be prepared!* it cries. And then again. And again. But for what? Here is a mystery: neither the body nor the sacrament knows. There is no knowledge. There is only a sense of something unknown.

THE UNPREPARING

There is one exception. If one lives long enough, if the body grows old, ears and nose full of hair, if the spirit becomes tired, if the heart has mellowed or learned to let go, similar changes sometimes take place in the sacrament. The sacrament starts to let go of its spin and to acquire a unique direction. Having sought for so long, it finally finds a focal point. It fixates. And it feels, at last—body, soul, and mind—that future toward which it now points.

In these last days, anticipation is unceasing. A nag. The body that once possessed the sacrament now feels as if it is the one who has been possessed. Perhaps it was this way all along. The former vigilance has departed. There is no preparation to complete. For that toward which the body and that toward which the sacrament has been pointing, arrives.

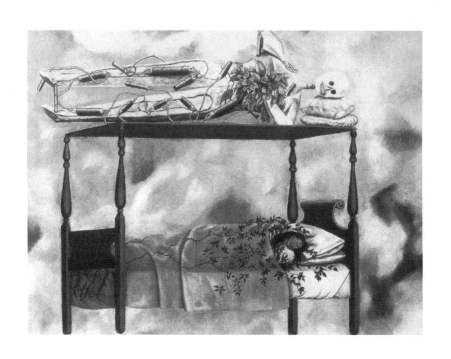

CHAPTER SIX

Liz, Pete, and the Things We Do for Love

Peter was a rough guy when they met. She knew they had no business together. Liz and this man. He had seven years on her, which at eighteen and twenty-five raised more than a few eyebrows. To say her dad didn't care for him would be too generous. Liz's dad hated Pete—hated his tattoos, hated his opinions, hated the way he treated his baby girl Liz. Pete was angry and moody. Pete could be lazy, in the winter he laid on the couch all day, getting fat. Though, the night they met Pete looked so good to Liz. There he was sitting across the bar, drinking beer after beer. He was wild and free. He looked strong and healthy burning down the Camels.

Even after she knew it was a mistake Liz was drawn to Pete. It didn't matter that his drinking was out of hand, his cheating was out of hand, the violence was out of hand. He was hard to leave, especially once their daughter was born. But eventually it got to be too much. Liz still loved him, she didn't know why, but it couldn't go on the way it was going and so she left.

That didn't mean that the relationship was over. Liz still saw Pete regularly. Despite everything he was a committed and involved dad. He took the girl every other weekend and on Tuesday nights. He was around for her softball games and flute recitals. He might not have been the man Liz deserved but he tried to be the father their baby girl needed. He was still a rough guy. Big and burly, Liz hated how he would pick their daughter up on his Harley. She was terrified they might get in an accident, that her little one might get hurt. If she was honest, Liz worried Pete might get hurt as well.

She knew there wasn't any point in arguing with him to pick her up in the car. She knew he loved to see the look on their daughter's face as he rolled up in the screaming machine. How could she not let their daughter go for a ride with her father? Liz remembered how much she had loved being on the back of that bike.

As the years went by the bike showed up less often. When Liz asked him why he didn't ride the Harley to pick up their not so little girl anymore he said he thought it was too dangerous. He didn't want her to get hurt. Over the years the big tattooed arms shrunk and jiggled, and his belly grew. Less beer and more diet coke. Less late nights and more early mornings. Liz met other fellas through the years and he certainly met other women, but nothing seemed to stick. When Liz's dad got sick, Pete was there. She was shocked he was there. Thirty years of hatred set aside. Decades of screaming matches, of cops called, water under the bridge. If she had been paying attention Liz should have seen it coming. Over the years they had softened toward each other. Liz's dad and Pete had spent enough graduations, holidays, and birthday parties together to get used to one another, eventually sort of liking each other. Either way they were fixtures in one another's lives. When Liz's dad got sick Pete showed up.

By this point their daughter had a baby girl of her own. Liz helped out with the baby every day while her daughter was at work. Pete stepped in and took over the babysitting duties while Liz attended to her father. This worked for a while until Liz hurt her back, and then the care for the old man was left to Pete. This man who once despised his father-in-law now found himself feeding the man, and changing him, washing his ex-father-in-law up. The two fellas would sit around and talk. Watch old westerns, or the Bears game. The past wasn't gone, it sat between them. But need and time dulled sharp edges.

When Liz's dad finally croaked, Pete was with him, and if he didn't shed a tear Pete's eyes certainly welled up. This act of kindness had bound Pete and Liz to each other once again. After a while he moved back in with her. Pete had his own place and kept up with the rent, but most of his time was spent with Liz. Their daughter was leery of it all but glad to be able to visit both at once, it certainly made the holidays easier. It went on like this for years. The two fell into a rhythm of being together. The rough and tough guy became an old man, who was far from tough. His sagging flesh made the old tattoos indecipherable. The motorcycle was sold. He wore track pants and white T-shirts instead of the leather jackets and blue jeans. Years of muffler-less riding and rock and roll stole most of his hearing. Hard living made his knees weak such that he had to use a walker. Liz found all of this endearing.

Eventually macular degeneration set in and Pete became largely blind. This, along with his other illness, meant Pete was dependent on Liz for help with most basic activities. His apartment was given up. The two, while still divorced, were back together under one roof. They had their fights, but the violence and the passion was gone, replaced by forgiveness and comfort. Liz didn't hesitate to remind Pete of the old days and his wild ways. On some level she missed the old wild Pete, but she loved him so much more now. The two spent most days sitting in the living room. Each had their own chair, and covered themselves with their own blankets. His had the Bear's logo all over it; her's had pictures of the two of them together. Their daughter had it made. Liz would cook, he would work out in the garden with Liz's help. Sometimes they listened to music. Old 45s from the days that they met, but most of the time they just watched TV, largely indifferent to the show, just happy to be together. The giant rottweiler they shared would shove himself up on the Lazy Boy with Pete for most of the day. It was so sweet that even the word "hate" Pete had tattooed across his knuckles was somehow cute, like a big guy named Tiny.

In their youth their love or maybe their infatuation was unsteady. It was a trek up and then a fall down mountains, but they had now come to a long plain of gentle, pervasive care. Their love was such that one didn't really know where one began and the other ended. Either one on their own couldn't face a single day, but together in their own way they learned to make it through. The bed wasn't the same thing as it had been for them. Their bed was no longer the seat of passion and sorrow. The pillows weren't full of sweat and tears. The bed was only for comfort and rest. They lay in it every night, holding each other's hands. Her fingers obscuring his ugly, faded tattoo.

Each night they slept hand in hand. Her CPAP machine screaming away, him getting up every hour to use the bedside commode. It wasn't a calm and peaceful evening but they were glad to be together in that bed—until they couldn't be. Pete had a fall one day. His vision being what it was he had many falls, only with this one he hit his head. It didn't seem that bad at first. Liz was able to get him up and onto the couch. She knew how much he hated the hospital; she didn't want to call the paramedics. It seemed like he was getting better. The headache subsided, he was making sense. "Leave me alone woman, I'm just tired." He was joking, and he wasn't just tired. There was a bleed in his brain and slowly cells were dying on the far side of that bleed, starving and unnourished. When he slept on the couch and didn't wake up in the morning Liz finally called the ambulance.

At the hospital Liz was told that, yes the brain injury had done damage, but Pete had a host of other issues that were the real problem. The usual suspects, diabetes and high blood pressure. More than likely he had an undiagnosed cancer. A shadow could be seen in the scans of his brain. The image was consistent with malignancy. She could have them run tests. They could cut him open and do a biopsy. The doctor said they could also do radiation or chemo, but most likely, due to the size and location of the tumor as well as Pete's health, this would be ineffective. There was a good chance the tumor was the cause of the fall in the first place.

Pete fought in the bed. He didn't really wake up but he thrashed and pulled out his catheter. The doctors gave him sedating medications, put mittens on his hands and soft restraints on his arms. Liz knew it wasn't discomfort or disorientation that was making him so aggressive. He was an independent person. His entire life Pete had prided himself on being able to handle his own issues. He didn't need anybody else's help and he didn't want it. Of course she had been leading him around the house for years, but she wasn't someone else, she hadn't been someone else for all those years. Liz knew what he wanted, she knew what he needed even if he didn't say it, even if he didn't know it. He wanted to go home. He wanted to be at the place he knew. He wanted to be with his music, his chair, the dog, her. She took him home on hospice care. The doctors wanted him to stay a little longer, but Liz wasn't having it.

It didn't take long at the house before they set up a hospital bed in the living room. They had to. The first couple of days after they got back Pete slept in the bed with Liz. He didn't say anything, didn't seem to know what was going on. He just laid in the bed next to her, hand in hand. If she had to get up for a minute to attend to something else he would reach out for her, and she'd come rushing back. His sleep was messed up. He rested during the day and was up most of the night. This meant that Liz hardly got any sleep at all; it wore on her, but she didn't let on. Their daughter came when she could. But she worked and had the little kid so it was hard.

The hospice staff was good. They helped Liz with cleaning and bathing Pete. They provided medications and even got Liz a part-time caregiver from the Department on Aging. Liz should have used the time the caregiver was there to sleep, to catch up on her rest, but she was too worried about Pete. She was always watching what the caregiver was doing. Never leaving her alone. Pete was skinny now but still tall and strong. Reflexively he fought against the people who tried to care for him, and he fell out of the bed regularly. Not only that, but when he had accidents in the bed or when he sweated through the sheets or anything else that required changing linens, the strain of moving him was too much on the caregiver's and Liz's backs. Reluctantly Liz got a hospital bed and put it in the living room. At night when she slept without him she could almost feel him holding her hand, and when she realized he wasn't there her heart sank. After a day or two she started sleeping out on the couch next to him.

Time went by that way for a while. Medications changed, some drugs dialed up, some backed off. They added new drugs and replaced old ones. Eventually they found a regimen that seemed to work, that maintained a status quo and even helped him sleep. The problem was the medications required a large amount of opioids. They worked well enough on his pain; they helped keep him calm. This, in turn, allowed Liz to get that rest. But over time, as Pete's system adapted to the drugs, the dosage had to go up. As it did some side effects began to show themselves.

Opioids have a number of negative side effects: addiction and confusion, nausea, slowing down of the basic systems of the body causing a massive wave of misery, crime and homelessness for large swaths of the American population. One of the less glamorous side effects is constipation. Opioids are going to plug a person up good. What else is going to plug a person up is not moving. If you lay in bed all day long it's not just you that goes still. Add to that limited fluid intake and you have a recipe for binding up the digestive tract. Stool softeners are often given along with the opioids in order to avoid this effect, but like all medications there are limits to their effectiveness. Those limits showed themselves and found Pete with concrete in his guts.

Liz noticed it first. She knew everything that went on with Pete. She kept meticulous notes of his blood pressure, his respiration, his pulse and oxygen levels, and of course his leavings. Everything that went in or out of the man was observed and noted. When stuff stopped coming out Liz paid attention. She told the nurse who upped the stool softener to no avail. The next visit the nurse had to give a suppository. It was uncomfortable for the nurse lifting up Pete's flesh and inserting the capsule in front of Liz, who refused to leave the room. But it was more uncomfortable for Liz as she knew how Pete would feel. Pete was a pile of drooping flesh and bone and problems to the nurse, she didn't know the wild tough-guy biker he had been. The nurse had no idea what it must have felt like to Pete, a man who believed himself capable of anything in his prime, to have lost the ability to even defecate, to need a stranger to insert a capsule into his anus so he could just have a bowel movement. The horror he would feel at it, the shame, Liz knew.

Pete, for his part, reached out during the process. He moaned and jerked. Liz had been told to medicate him ahead of time to weaken Pete's body for the fight, but he certainly was not happy about the turn of events. Liz and Pete both were heartbroken. Pete had lived his entire life one way and then in the last years had to give up so much of his independence; that was hard enough, but now this shame of shame. He couldn't even properly shit himself. He couldn't use a diaper like a baby. Whoever he was anymore, whatever was left of the old wild man, couldn't live with the shame of it. Liz saw this and vowed not to let it happen again.

The medication worked. The stool passed and Liz was able to get Pete cleaned up with help of their daughter. After that she was on top of Pete's bowels. She made sure that he kept up with his stool softener, that he ate the right foods, when he could eat, because that would help the waste move along. It worked, things moved along smoothly, then Liz's brother died.

She went to the funeral; she didn't want to, but life is full of hard choices. The funeral was down in Florida where her brother had retired. Their daughter couldn't watch Pete because of her baby and work, but there was a provision in the hospice contract that provided a five-day "respite" stay in a nursing home. It seemed like a good option. The social worker set it up. Pete left on a Friday and came back on Monday afternoon, not even using the full five days of the benefit. Pete left in bad shape and he came back much, much worse.

When the ambulance arrived with him on that Monday Liz broke down in tears. What color he had was drained. What meat was on his bones had been eaten away. His clothes were gone, disappeared into the collective pot of clothing passed from patient to patient at the nursing home, which was a shame because she sent him in his favorite Lynyrd Skynyrd T-shirt, the one from the concert they went to when they were still just kids. It was their third or fourth date depending on how you reckon what's a date or not. It was presently being worn by Mary, a confused former choir director who believed deeply that rock and roll was the devil's music.

Pete looked tiny. He was thin before he left but to Liz he was always a big man—not now. He didn't have softened edges; he was squished flat. Empty. Liz would hardly recognize him if not for the faded ink on his arms and knuckles. Even that looked more faded and more distorted. The ambulance drivers helped to get Pete back into the hospital bed. They lifted him from the stretcher to the bed like they were moving a Fabergé egg, like he was something small and precious that might break at any moment. This was a man who had once drunk a bottle of Jack in one afternoon and proceeded to ride his Harley in a lightning storm down the side of a mountain. This was a man who looked for trouble, who had survived in the jungles of Vietnam and on the back streets of America, even spent some time behind bars. None of that had broken him, going blind hadn't broken him. Even with his loss of ability to take care of himself somehow he still was there, beaten but unbroken. No longer. What returned from the nursing home was a broken man, maybe less than that.

Pete was contracted. His legs had pulled into his chest, frozen in the fetal position. The ambulance driver had been kind enough to place a pillow between his legs to keep them from rubbing up against each other, causing a sore to develop. They took their pillow back as Liz slipped one of theirs in its place. Liz strained to hold Pete's legs apart long enough to get the pillow in between his knees. Pete's hands were curled up in balls, the fingertips digging into his palms. Everything about Pete was rigid and stiff. When Liz tried to move him it felt like he might break in two, that his femur could snap like uncooked pasta. She tried to work his hands apart. She massaged them with oil and lavender. They might have been softer after her spa treatment but he still squeezed tight. Those hands had squeezed the handlebars on his chopper, had held their daughter's hand when they walked across the street, on more than one occasion those hands had squeezed Liz's arm in anger. Now they dug into each other leaving behind angry-looking grooves. If the man had any strength left at all it was being spent torturing himself. On top of this, he was impacted.

He hadn't gotten his stool softener while at the nursing home. It was someone's oversight. A simple mistake, really, with a drug that didn't seem like a big deal to anyone—anyone but Liz and Pete. When Liz went to change his diaper about half an hour after he arrived, she noticed. Getting the old diaper off Pete's legs tucked in the fetal position was difficult, but he had been given his pain meds when he arrived, which did allow the body to loosen up some. She was able to get the old diaper off. It was dry and it was clean. Not so much a smear of residue. But as she changed him she could see that even through the medication he was in pain. He grimaced and even let out a little moan as she rolled him around. His face contorted in on itself. She had seen that face before. Liz knew what it was. She knew he couldn't pass his stool.

The body is an object in motion all the time. Even the most sedentary person is constantly pumping blood, firing neurons, expanding and contracting their lungs. To live is to move; most of that motion we have no idea about. The conscious human is but a small part of the genius that keeps us running. But to stay in motion all that time requires input and output. When one isn't fed the machine breaks down, when one can't remove the waste the machine breaks down. When the machine breaks down it hurts. It hurts even people who seem beyond hurt. It hurts the medicated, the comatose, and it hurts the dying. Liz couldn't stand to see Pete in such pain. It tore at her soul to watch the man struggle to simply live. To remain as something in motion in this world.

Liz lifted up his butt cheek, there wasn't much cheek left. She did so gingerly as a red sore had begun to form on his coccyx and she worried it might be tender. She looked into that part of a human where nobody looks, that Holy of Holies. Those parts we keep separate from nearly all, even from ourselves. It felt to her like a violation, like she was somehow breaking a rule, a taboo so basic that it didn't need to be spelled out or expounded upon. She looked in as if she were looking between her fingers at some unnamed terror. What she saw angered her but didn't surprise her.

It was there, right at the end of his rectum. Human feces, waste, that which remains when all that is good and wholesome and nourishing is squeezed out, when the things of value have been extracted and consumed, what remains when all else is gone. It was there pushing on his flesh. On the delicate space that forms the border between us and the world. One of the human body's porous places where the outside can get in and what's inside fights to get out. There in this weak spot the shit backed up. Liz knew what had to be done.

Liz was no nurse, but Liz had raised her baby daughter and so she knew about this dirtiest aspect of human existence. She had wiped her fair share of behinds. She, like all of us, understood the importance of defecation. She would spend about ninety-two days of her life, the average amount of time for an average person, on the john. She knew stomach pains and gas. She had the occasional bout of diarrhea. Back when they were first married, when Pete had been mean and abusive, she had developed bleeding issues and ulcers. She had hemorrhoids occasionally, and they hurt. She hid the Tucks pads in the back of the bathroom cabinet. Liz was as affected by her digestive system as anyone. Liz, like all of us, knew to keep it to herself. She knew that what she did in the bathroom, as important as it was to her life and wellbeing, was nobody else's business. She wanted to keep it that way. Liz also did what she could to stay out of other people's bathroom issues.

In Pete's case some of this had already been suspended. She had already been caring for him. She cleaned up when he crapped all over himself. She washed the stained sheets and scrubbed the floor. There was a time before he fell when Pete had been unable to get to the bathroom and had diarrhea so bad that it overflowed his pants and crawled all the way up his back. There was so much of the fetid fluid that Liz had to wash it out of his hair. Their mattress was forever stained after that, a physical reminder of the shame he felt. Much of the mystery between Pete and Liz had gone out of the window simply because of need. But this was something different. As she looked into the body of her lover, her tormentor, her partner, her friend, she realized that she was going to have to physically remove the shit.

She could have called the hospice nurse. Maybe she should have, but she knew what it would be like for him to have a stranger help. She was heartbroken enough by what had become of Pete in the nursing home. The thought of another person doing to him what she was about to do was too much, neither she nor he could bear it. Liz knew even her assisting him would break Pete's spirit, but a stranger? A stranger digitally removing Pete's waste wouldn't kill him, it would erase who he was altogether. She would rather put a pillow over his face than put him through that shame, so Liz did what she had to do.

She grabbed a glove and put it on, slowly. Once it was on she realized that she would need something to make the process easier. Liz took the glove off, went to the bathroom and dug around in the drawers. It took her five minutes to find the old jar of Vaseline that had been there since her father was alive. Liz took it out and looked all over the jar for an expiration date. She didn't know if Vaseline expired but she wanted to be sure it didn't. She didn't see a date. She uncrewed the lid and dipped a finger into the thick, oily substance. She rubbed it on the pointer finger on her right hand until it was good and lubed up. As soon as it was, Liz realized she didn't have a glove on. It took a minute or two to wipe the Vaseline off her finger.

Liz took the jar into the living room where Pete lay on his side uncovered. His nakedness exposed to the world.

Liz grabbed another glove and pulled it on. It ripped; she grabbed another. Once it was on she took the same pointer finger she had lubed up before and stuck it down deep into the Vaseline. She formed a "J" with her finger, snagging a good glob of the lube while pulling it out of the bottle. Liz moved slowly and deliberately, rubbing the Vaseline all over her finger. She still had only a vague idea of what was going to happen next. She had maybe heard of a disimpaction. She had a hazy memory of helping a puppy years before to ease out a particularly hard poop, but this was largely uncharted territory for her.

A nurse is trained to disimpact a person. The nurse is taught a process and procedure, and warning signs that what they are doing might be going too far or not far enough. They practice and are given pointers by more experienced nurses. Liz did not have the benefit of any of that. She was working out of desperation and something like common sense. She saw the problem and addressed it as best she could. Liz again lifted up the deflated flesh of her ex-husband's butt cheek and looked inside.

It was still there, bulging against the flesh, trying to get out but unable to squeeze through. Liz closed her eyes, trying to feel her way around. By not looking it felt like she was giving Pete some amount of privacy, and as such dignity. But the gloves and the Vaseline limited her dexterity. She couldn't move by feel, she had to look and so she did. She placed her pointer finger on the hole. With her other hand and her middle finger on the working hand she separated the flesh. Pete let out a slight moan as the waste appeared before her. The hard brown waste, a tormentor inside the man she loved. Liz wanted to move quickly, to rip the evil out, to exorcise that demon. Not only that but she wanted to hasten the end of the horrible task, though she knew she couldn't. Liz knew how fragile Pete was and didn't want to cause any new damage.

Gently she touched the fecal material. It gave little and crumbled slightly but mostly stood hard as a rock. She knew she had to get around the top and behind it. She placed her gloved and lubed finger at the top of his anal opening. Slowly she worked her finger into the cavity, creating a space between the flesh and waste. Pete moaned again in pain. An arm, which hadn't moved since he returned, reached out desperately at her as if to try and stop what was happening. She dropped the cheek she was holding and grabbed his hand with her free hand, holding it as she tried to continue working the inserted finger. She found this impossible with the flesh collapsed on top of her hand. Liz gently stroked Pete's reaching fingers. "Shush, shush," she said. "It's okay honey, this will make you feel better I promise. Just let me do this." Pete continued to moan but his hand stopped reaching and contracted back into his chest. Liz again lifted the flesh of his cheek and she continued her task.

Liz worked her finger around the outside of the impaction and the flesh. Trying to create space. She felt something through the glove. The feeling was muted by the latex but it was obviously hot and wet, she looked again at her glove and saw the bright ruby red blood from a broken vessel dripping onto her down her glove. Liz pulled her hand out instinctively and took a step back, looking at the blood. Her eyes welled up. She had harmed him. She was trying to help but she had hurt Pete. She was trying to stop the pain but had caused some instead. She took off the glove, covered him up and walked around to the other side of the bed. Kneeling down so her head was close to his.

"I'm so sorry baby, I didn't mean to hurt you. I just didn't know what else to do." The words seemed almost familiar as she said them. She had heard them from him many times before. She put her forehead against his and took a deep breath. He was curled up tighter than before, his brow more furrowed, the pain was still there. She hadn't finished the task and she knew she had to now. She had gone too far. The blood had to be worth something. The look of anguish on Pete's face demanded that she finish the job.

Liz steadied herself, looked Pete in the eyes and swore she saw some recognition there, maybe even permission, or perhaps that's just what she wanted to see. "Okay honey, I'm gonna finish the job." She stood up off her knees and walked around behind Pete lifting the sheet she had tossed over him. She reached for new gloves; the box was empty. She looked for another box but there weren't any where she normally left them. She checked the closet, none there. Liz remembered that the nurse had ordered new supplies but said the delivery company was backed up and they wouldn't get there for another two days. Liz thought about going to the store, but one look at Pete and she knew she couldn't leave him alone. She panicked. "Shit," she shouted loud enough the neighbors heard it but not so loud they did anything about it. No sooner had the noise left her lips than Liz looked wide-eyed at Pete, afraid that her outburst might have frightened him. His furrowed brow had not changed one way or the other.

Liz knew what she had to do. She was loath to do it, but there was no other option. She thought about putting a Ziplock bag or plastic wrap over her hand, but the gloves had done enough to limit her dexterity and they were designed to be worked with. She breathed deep and sighed on the way out. "Good job Lizzy, way to go on this one." She grabbed the Vaseline and rubbed it around her naked pointer finger for the second time in one day. "Funny," she thought she never would have imagined even using the lubricant let alone twice in a day on the same digit. "Okay you can do this babe," Liz said to herself as she returned to her work.

It's amazing how quick a person can gain muscle memory for an action. What took her a minute to do only ten minutes before now she did in five seconds. Lifting up his cheek and exposing the swollen flesh. There was a little redness and drop of dried blood where she had torn the skin before, but nothing more. A tiny bit of feces had actually broken free and was sitting on the sheet under Pete. Again she placed her finger near the top of the opening, trying to avoid the wound. It was hard to do but without gloves she could feel the gap between the opening and the waste. Again she wiggled her finger into the space between. Slower this time to avoid damage. It was gross feeling the dry hard shit against the impossibly sensitive skin of her finger tip. A smell released this time. The horrible stink of illness and stagnant feces. The build up behind the blockage. Despite her attempts to steel herself, despite her intense concentration, a wave of nausea bubbled up in Liz's stomach. She choked it down for now, but it did not subside.

Liz grit her teeth, as did Pete. She bent her finger on top of itself and down into the impaction. Gouging a hole through the hard dry surface and into the soft inside. She gulped down vomit as she brought the finger up again, and then stabbed into the foul blockage again. She was breaking up the jam little by little. Once it was sufficiently broken down she pulled out a piece and then stuck her finger back in. There was more room now and she was able to break up more and more of the impaction with each subsequent stab. A few drops of blood mingled with the waste she extracted.

Over and over again she swallowed down the sick. After the first hunk was removed more of the build up came down. Pete's digestive tract began to function again. Muscles contracted and brought more and more waste to the anus. It was softer but still too hard for Pete to pass on his own. Liz kept at it. She kept digging into her ex-husband's hidden places for the next half an hour. Mining the horrible, the leavings and illness trapped for so long in the man. She freed the sickness and stink from his body. Little by little, over and over, she removed more waste than she thought a person could have in them. Liz hadn't brought a diaper or a garbage bag to put the foul in so she simply piled it on the bed, until that became too much. Then she piled it on the bedside table. It was an old table, a wedding gift from when they were first married. It would be easy enough to clean and then could be gotten rid of when this was all over.

It kept coming, as if it had been up there his entire life, more and more. The nausea didn't let up for Liz. Her hands were covered. The feces had worked its way under her nail bed, into the folds of her knuckles, around the wedding band she had only recently started wearing again. Pete was no longer moaning, in fact his rigid body seemed to be relaxing. Calming. Finding peace as the vile waste continued to flow out of him, until finally it stopped. Liz stepped back sick and sweating. She didn't know if ten minutes or an hour had passed. She wiped her brow with the wrong hand, which she immediately regretted. The feeling of the wet smear on her forehead sent Liz to the bathroom where finally she released the contents of her stomach. She washed her hands and her face with scalding water. She took off her shirt and pants.

Liz walked back into the room in her underwear. Pete was still on his side, his backside pointing at her. Liz cleaned him up. She filled up a bucket of warm water in the kitchen sink. She slowly bathed his relaxing body. She was deliberate and thorough. When Liz was done, Pete was the cleanest he had been in months. She stripped the bed leaving Pete laying directly on the mattress. She got a garbage bag, paper towels, and a can of Lysol and cleaned up the bedside table. She was right, it cleaned up fast. The next day their daughter would take the table to Goodwill.

Liz found a diaper and redressed her husband. She put a fresh shirt on him and fresh sheets on top of him. She sprayed the room with Febreze and opened the window. Liz stepped back and looked at her Pete. He looked calm. He didn't look strong; he didn't look like the wild man she met. He did look a little like the man who held their baby girl, the man who sat with her dying father. He looked calm and relaxed. The tension was gone. Liz smiled to herself and went to take a shower.

Liz let the hot water run over her. Despite aching knees, she lowered herself down into the tub and sat in the stream for a while. The water was scalding but she didn't mind. She let it pour over her until it ran cool. Then she let the cool water run until it was too cold to sit in. The water worked its way down into her muscles and joints. It relieved her anxiety and took away her pain. The white noise of the shower allowed her mind to wander, back to the night they met, back to the baby he held, back to long days sitting on their chairs. Then her thoughts drifted to nothing, simple exhausted emptiness. After a lifetime she stood up, shivering. Liz shut off the shower. The house was silent except for a robin singing outside the window. Liz grabbed a towel and dried off.

She brushed her teeth and combed her hair straight. Liz looked at herself in the mirror, she knew who she was, and right now at least she was happy with that. When she walked into the other room it took only one look to know what had happened. Pete was dead. The relief, the moment of comfort, it was enough for him to let go of it all. He drifted off while she was in the shower. Maybe he didn't want her to see him go, maybe he chose that moment, or maybe it just worked out that way. She saw his half open eyes and half open mouth. His clean body under a clean sheet. The room had aired out. While there was a dead body, there was no scent of death. Liz knelt down next to Pete and stroked his hair.

She had been told what to do next. She knew she would have to call hospice. The hospice would send out someone to pronounce Pete dead, but she didn't feel like calling just then. She didn't feel like letting strangers in. Like hosting them as they did their business. She just wanted a moment alone with Pete. A second between them, past life, death, and illness. Without thinking she climbed into the hospital bed with him. The air mattress stuck to her flesh as she scooted in. It was tight, hardly enough room for both of them. Liz curled up into Pete. Her head rested on his shoulder. Her hand found his and held on tight enough for the both of them, his knuckles enwrapped by her clean and soft flesh. Liz drifted off to sleep.

Interlude

Passing Through, Part One: Rose & Jack

White gloves. White lace. Slender cigarettes in holders made of jade. Easter hats, Easter smiles. Here. In highest heavens. Echelons above. Where every day is a glorious day. The day of resurrection.

Every resurrection demands a feast. And feasting we meet her. On a ship, she's surrounded. By gasping legs, believing eyes. Aglaze, they hurry down the hill to meet her. *The tomb is empty. The tomb is empty! The tomb is empty!* they say. She finds this hard to believe.

Rose is her name. And this is the story of her coming of age. An event marked not by the passage of time, but by a passing-through. An adventure. A journey. A quest. From one world. To another. And back.

The quest begins as all quests do, kettles screaming, a hero steeped in discontent. Yearning. Pining. Flailing on floors. *Is this all? Is this all? Is this really all there is?* The newspapers seem to bear witness to the contrary. As do the periodicals. Oh! The periodicals! How they reveal ways of living, ways of believing, ways so sweetly distinct from our own. Rose reads all of them aflush. Captivated. Taken by the beauty of worlds yet to be. Taken, yet feeling captive in her own.

And *this*. The feasting. The costumes. The smiles, frozen. This whole celebratory scene. This manifestation of the paradisiacal dream of preceding generations: to Rose, this all is suffocating. A charade. A yawn. A procession, mandatory, that she must join. Squinting through holes in a mask made for another's eyes. Must she accept this? The end of a rainbow born of another's storm?

Among the Resurrected, there is a place known as hell, a smoldering lake set aside for the less-than-human. A place of cages for evil beasts and torturous contraptions prepared for the licentious, the pick-pockets, the masturbators, and the undivine. The dregs of the universe. Every place has a hell. Every city. Every town. Every body. Every park, port, and parcel.

A ship's hell is located inside and at its bottom. This is where Rose's quest will take her. And it is where she'll be met with surprise. For it is in hell, in introduction after introduction, in encounter after encounter, in drink, after drink, after dance, that Rose comes slowly to realize that, indeed, in hell there are strong scents. But, contrary to explorers' reports, they are not sulfuric. There are screams. But their source is delight. Rose comes to realize about hell that which is true of every prison. Hell is not filled with demons. But with the poor.

Hell is also the place where, hidden from heaven's evil eye, Rose will learn to shout. To sing. To dance. It is the place where all that she'd been forced to tie down or to pack into a bundle on her back would be released, opened, exposed, and transformed. Converted into the fuel that would feed the fire that would forge the person she would soon become. And all of this in hell.

Quests are seldom taken all alone. Companions are picked up along the way, breathing in campfire and canned goods smoking beneath the midnight skies. Rose found a companion of her own on her quest. Someone who was willing to walk along. Someone who had been to hell (and hells) before. Enter: Jack.

Jack is a derivative of the name John. In its meaning, it is a name that bears witness to God's glory and grace. In this story of Rose's coming of age, this is what Jack is. A benediction. A blessing. A gift. Chains fall to the floor when he and Rose embrace. Her freedom incarnate in sweet handsome flesh. Her dreams of new worlds, in caresses, made complete. It is unknown whether Dante kissed Virgil while spelunking in the Inferno. But if he did, what a wonderful story that would be!

In the era of black-and-white television, there was no shortage of programming about cowboys, farmers, and ranchers (many of them sanitizing or simplifying life in the field or on the range, omitting accounts of forced displacements and genocides that had gained them these lands not many generations before).

In nearly all of these programs, there came a moment in which the parent was called to teach a child about the importance of maintaining the anonymity of the animals contained in one's barnyard. To sacrifice a cow whom one has given a name—let's say Buttercup—even if the promised result at the other end of the killing is sweet and glorious steak, feels very much to every child like murdering a beloved household pet. It is senseless. Awful. Stupid. And mean. It is detestable and, as such, worthy of indignant protestations. *I will eat nothing but Brussels sprouts and potatoes for the rest of my life!*, a child in the program declares, refusing to be domesticated. *This is the sacrifice I wish to make. To save Buttercup, my friend, my sibling, I will start a meat strike!*

It is not until a certain skill is acquired and then developed over decades, by way of practice and parental indoctrination, that the child will be able both to form attachments *and* to accept an order of things in which the clear role of the child and the child's family is not only to feed, to clean, and to care for Buttercup, but also to kill her, stroking her coat, staring into hamburger eyes.

In these programs, the killing itself is portrayed as somber and lamentable. There are sympathetic orchestras. The moments in which the deed is committed are never shown on the screen. Only the child before and then a fade to gray. And yet, the whole event is presented also as a turning point. A rite of passage. And (as for Rose) a coming of age.

To hear the cries of Buttercup, to divert them from the heart, and to sequester them in a forgotten place, we learn—to care for a creature and simultaneously to plot its demise: this is what it means to have reached one's maturation. This is what it means to have become a well-adjusted adult.

Near the end of *Titanic* (the movie that tells the story of Rose) we find Rose sitting in a chair, reflecting. The TV audience is riveted by her testimony about her quest and about the salvation that she found in the body of Jack. The story, however, is bittersweet. For, while she was saved, Jack drowned in the crash.

The story portrayed in *Titanic* is born from an ideology commonly known as Hollywood Communism, an ideology that has been expounded upon, in great length, by philosopher Slavoj Žižek.[1] The *communism* portion of this term points toward the presumed class solidarity portrayed in Rose's descent and alleged conversion to the poor while she is in hell. *Hollywood* highlights the centering of a bourgeois protagonist or *hero* whose ending is almost always bound to be a happy one. In the course of the film, of course, we learn that Rose's solidarity is both inauthentic and fleeting. It is a protest selfie, screaming *common cause* with the masses, feeling

---

1. See Žižek, *Pervert's Guide to Ideology.*

personally uplifted, and then returning to a gated community, tipping the security guard, sunglasses down, while racing by.

Said differently, despite the momentary illusion of intimacy that Rose perceived as taking place between herself and the underclasses, when the ice strikes, it is brought to the surface that these *intimacies* are, in actuality, only sophisticated expressions of distance and estrangement. There is no solidarity. There is no uprising (for her). No substantive change or transformation for good. All ends as it had always been. White gloves. White lace. Slender cigarettes in holders made of jade.

The poor, the proletariat, Jack? None of these become her comrades, none her community. Or, said better, she never becomes theirs. Rather, they become a tool for her use. Made to give her meaning. Existing for the sake of her adventure and the subsequent airing of a prime time story. A sacrifice, their lives were given so that she, and all those who dwell in the highest heavens, might be saved.

Interlude

Passing Through, Part Two: Chōra

É skhatos means *end* or *last* in Greek. For this reason, theologians have come to call the study of end things *eschatology*. The world of eschatological thinking has long been preoccupied with the apocalyptic *end* of the world, the *conclusion* of time as we know it, a rapture, a reign, a throne, a dragon with many heads, and being Left Behind™. The sources for eschatology, scriptural and noncanonical, are many—as are the eschatological conversations to be had.

One of those conversations was planted and watered by theologian and poet, Vítor Westhelle. Westhelle asked two compelling questions. *What if, when Jesus said the end was near, he meant not "near in time," but, rather, "nearby in space?"* and *What if "at hand" means "so close you can touch it?"*

Said differently, Westhelle wondered aloud what it would look like for eschatologists to approach eschatology from a *spatial* rather than a *temporal* lens. When we do this, he found, a whole new world of understanding emerges. No longer must we look exclusively for the signs of the times, the inbreaking of God's future, or the end of the age. For now, we may also look for the signs of our *spaces*, the reign that is already *here*, nearby, adjacent, within, and at the ends, limits, and delineations of the places around and beyond us.[1]

As we seek to understand or evaluate the stories of Liz and Pete, Rose and Jack, there is one particular piece of Westhelle's spatialized eschatology that stands out as helpful. The anticipation of a coming *parousia*, that has often been marked by visions of sword-wielding, fire-breathing christs riding white horses and puking up every drop of lukewarm water, says

1. See Westhelle, *Eschatology and Space.*

Westhelle, for us may be replaced with an expectation of God's arrival in each and every encounter with each and every o/Other.[2]

That is to say, the *parousia*, or God's crossing *back* or re-presencing into our space and our time in a special way at the end of time (a common hope expressed in various pieties and eschatological frameworks), may be replaced in this frame by an emphasis on our crossing of *spaces*—or, perhaps better said—finding ourselves in the crossing from one place to another.

As every door has a threshold, so every place has a space of crossing between itself and the place at which we might arrive. These spaces between places Westhelle calls *chōratic*. Chōra is a Greek word holding a number of meanings. These include: to lie open, to listen, to be attentive, or to be ready to receive.[3] Every crossing from one place into another is chōratic, Westhelle reports, because in every crossing from one place to another, in every transgression of a delineation, a barrier, a border, a fence, a body, there lies (in potentiality) the possibility of an experience of God's unveiling or apparition or presence *taking place* in one's encounter with (or one's crossing over into) one's o/Other. As we cross, open and attentive, listening and ready to receive, sometimes, in some places, there is God. So says Westhelle.[4]

2. My use of o/Other here is faithful to Westhelle's use.

3. Westhelle, *Church Event*, 128.

4. The chōratic itself is a Derridean concept adopted by Westhelle and used throughout his works (as is Westhelle's reference to the o/Other). It is especially helpful in thinking in post- and de-colonial frames regarding the "crossing" of the Atlantic and the countless encounters that ensue as a result. Perhaps his most explicit expression of what it means to "cross over" and encounter an Other while never perceiving one's other rightly, is found in Westhelle's essay, "Scientific Sight and Embodied Knowledges." Here, Westhelle describes colonizers' accounts of the indigenous peoples that they tortured and enslaved in what they would come to call the Americas. Though colonizers met fellow humans in quite vulnerable circumstances, their European (and eschatological) gaze was so ideologically rigid that they could not see the humans that stood just beyond it. Though a human was in front of them (and the meeting could have theoretically resulted in the "taking place" of Christ in human encounter and love) these Europeans saw only in stereotype. These were only "savages," they said. Here in the chōra, there was no salvation, but only bloodshed. At the same time, there were those present who drew the "specimens" that they spectated in "the Americas." They sent their sketches back to Europe where they were then printed, reprinted, and circulated throughout the colonized world for all to see. Caricatures, these colonizer-representations were received as science and fact and truth. This hardened the ideological lens of those who imbibed it—which in turn perpetuated the dehumanization, torture, and displacement of indigenous peoples that continues to this day. Womanist theologian, Emilie Townes, calls this process of

Of course, this does not mean that every encounter in every cross-ing is revelatory. On the contrary. Such encounters are not as common as we might think. As the prophets testify, just like the child who learns to funnel the cries of Buttercup away from her heart, so there are barriers within and around us that prevent us from perceiving the o/Other on our way—screaming, singing, or otherwise. Racism. Nationalism. Criminaliza-tion. White picket fences. Thick prison walls. Buzzing fluorescent nursing homes. All of these keep us from sensing our o/Other who is nearby and at hand. All of these keep our o/Other from sensing us. And so what hap-pens? Well, when we let these -isms shape our lenses, as a result, we end up perceiving the o/Other not as the o/Other but in the caricature or ste-reotype that those lenses have been shaped to perceive. A horror film's fun house mirror. Our senses sense a human. Through the lens, we perceive three-fifths. Our senses sense a neighbor. Through the lenses there is only an enemy. There is only a convict, a servant, a messiah, a sacrifice, a dog, a Samaritan.[5] Over time we don't even need the lenses anymore. Our eyes have adapted. The enemy is everywhere. Sinners: everyone.

We look but we do not see. We encounter but we never meet. We change course, but nothing metanoietic takes place. Because we've been conditioned. To distort the image of our o/Others. To see with fearful eyes. To pull triggers. To show we're well-adjusted, domesticated, civilized. Citi-zens of Rome. To accept that the world is as it is, the way that it will always be. This is what happened to Rose at the expense of Jack. And this is why the studio audience leaned in to listen and roared with applause.

---

caricature, dehumanization, and oppression, "the fantastic hegemonic imagination" and "the cultural production of evil." Today, and throughout history, she demonstrates, it is much more than sketches that prevent us from seeing the person across from us and the God/Other in the chōra.

Each wonder with us. Can we dream of an eschatology that perceives the Divine tak-ing place and open for embrace in our others, or will we doom ourselves to the repetition and perpetuation of the nightmare that is human history?

Westhelle, "Scientific Sight," 346–61; Townes, *Womanist Ethics*, 7, 45.

5. See Townes, *Womanist Ethics*, 8.

Interlude

Passing Through, Part Three: Liz & Pete

Liz's adventure may not have been as action-packed as the one told of Rose. No ship was sunk. No bodies drowned. No movie was created to showcase her life. Cinema material or not, however, Liz, too, had plenty of chōratic spaces to navigate. Three demand our attention now, each of them involving a recurring o/Other in Liz's life: her off-and-on love interest, Peter.

The first chōratic space in which Liz finds herself is the threshold that is every pub and bar. Past the jukebox. The vending machine. The menthols and Camel Lights. Past the dart boards. The beer spills. The nutshells on the floor. Here. In a sea of people, eyes meet. Ears warm, aflush. Lord! My Lord! Who is this man? Dangerous. Rebellious. Unchained. Huey Newton. James Dean. Andy Warhol. Zapatistas. Free. *Mine!* Liz breathes at the sight of him. *Mine! He must be mine! He must be mine for I, too, wish to be free.*

Of course, Liz does not see Peter. She sees a savior. That is to say, Liz sees that which she desires. Every drink he takes, every cigarette, every drunk drive, glasses steamed, windows down, is not a vice. Nor a wish for death. It is no spiral into shadows below. Each, rather, is *a slap in the face*, delivered to every head of every establishment. And to every status quo. To every oppressive and repressive structure in the world that has placed Liz and Peter here in this dive while—as the waddling bass in the background reminds them—the rich folks pass by eating in their fancy dining cars, probably drinking coffee and smoking fine cigars.

A nonconformist. An asphalt-cracking flower, stretching toward the sun. *Damn the Man!* he smiles. *Live hard. Play hard. I'll sleep when I'm dead.* A way. An escape. From the erosion. From the grind. From callus and blister. From work, work, work, work, work, and never enough for food, for medicine, for gas, for lights, for insurance, for payments then payments then payments again, for vacations (ha!), for movies, for ____.

Some say he is John the Baptist. And others, Elijah. Perhaps he is Jeremiah or one of the prophets. But Liz testifies to the truth: *You are the messiah! The child given from God.* And here, in his glorious presence, Liz, with all of her love, believes. *My rock*, he calls her. And so she will be. Until the *slaps* become directed toward her.

Much later, Liz finds herself in a second chōratic space. It is after his burial. That is: after she has banished him for many years. Resurrected, he appears at the threshold of her house. Feeble. And weak. A ghost. Disintegrating. Walking through the walls. A parousia. No sword. No horse. He is weak. And his weakness renders him lovable.

This crossing (which is also a return) gives birth to a home of sorts. Or at least something consensual. It is markedly different from what it was before. For this time, Liz knows Pete has not come to save.

Her soteriological urge is abnormally strong, it seems. Feeling it, Liz is compelled to do some meditating. As she sits beneath the tree, for minutes, for days, an ethic of reciprocity begins to blossom. *I was harmed. And now I am safe. Being safe, I must now save others.* Her heart declares this—and trembles. I must save. And I will begin with Pete, for he is a widow. He is a beggar, a leper. He is a woman with a hemorrhage whose son has also died. He has been beaten by robbers on the side of the road. He is hungry and I gave him something to eat. In prison, and I visited. *It was not Peter who came to save. It is I who has come to save him.*

Being a savior is hard work. There are always too many prayers and too little time to answer—even when you are not the savior of the whole world, but only of a household, a hospital bed, and a man plugged into medical machines. It is a job that never ends. And one that seldom feels chosen. Rather, life is a series of emergencies and mystical beeps, placing you on call, lamps lit, ready to respond, to take action, to fix whatever it is that is breaking or beeping—running low on batteries or running out of breath. Some have entertained angels without knowing it.

And so it is that, not by desire, but by circumstance, Liz finds herself at her third (and our final) chōratic crossing. There, by grace alone, a quest is granted, given, golden, as angels sing. *You are to go where none have gone before. Fear not. To guide you in the wilderness and through the night, I will send you a star.*

So Liz strains her back. And she remembers a book she read in grade four. *The Dutch Boy!* Plugging the holes of the dike. She laughs. This is like that—but in reverse. A finger. Wet. Damming back a vomitous flood. Dry to wet. Light to tunnels unknown.

Here. In this crossing, this chōra, this threshold leading into an o/Other who'd been dwelling so nearby for years; here inside the one upon whose skin her many masks had once alighted like a dove; here, inside the outsides that they shared; the messiahs she had seen: the gods in him and the gods in herself—the Warhols, the Newtons, the beggars, the lepers, the crowds, and all of the kids—all of them, every one of them, each and every-one dissolved. Raptured.

Caught up in the clouds.

A descent.

A trigger pulled.

When the smoke cleared and the bar lights came on, she met him, at last, for the first time. There he was. No leather. No hero. No Jack. No solidarity. No *the poor.* Just this. A human undressed, glorious-exposed. A mortal. Filled with the breath of the divine. It was a moment—and that is all—and in it, she loved him, truly, and with depth. There. In the crossing. In the chōra. In the space from an o/Other into one.

White gloves.

White lace.

Slender cigarettes in holders made of jade.

Today.

Is a day.

Of resurrection.

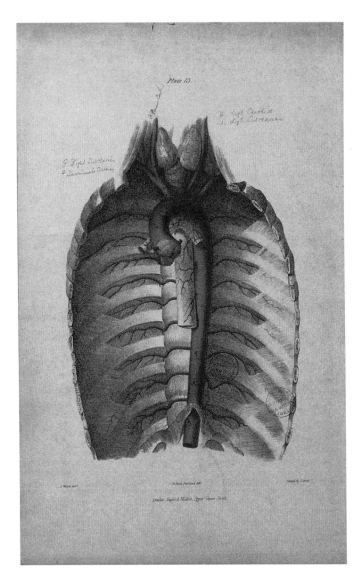

Plate 13.

CHAPTER SEVEN

Bill and the Strange Liturgy of CPR

The first day of paramedic school was designed to weed out the people who didn't belong there. Many of the students weren't going to pass the course, even among those who made it through the first day. Becoming a medic is surprisingly rigorous. It requires physical ability, mental capacity, a certain amount of poise and creativity. And paramedic school didn't always draw the best and the brightest. As such, many would wash out during the program. But before any of that can come into play the medic must be able to handle the basics of the job. The instructors, all medics themselves, knew that the job was going to put some pretty awful things in front of their students and the instructors had to be sure that these students could handle those awful things. It might be that someday one of the students now sitting in front of the instructor in class, would be sitting next to them as their partner in an ambulance. You want the person in the bus with you to know what they are doing. You have to trust they can get the job done.

A classic and time-tested way to weed people out of the program was to show them pictures of horrible accidents. If they couldn't handle a photo in a PowerPoint, if an image on a screen was going to stun them or make them sick, then being a medic probably wasn't going to be the right line of work for them. Bill remembered sitting in his seat watching the Power-Point. It started like the PowerPoint shown at the beginning of any class—a few slides about the schedule, class time, and dates. One or two that covered grading and attendance policies. There was a slide about the books they needed to buy, how well they needed to score on the various tests and quizzes to stay in the class. The hours of practical work they would be required to do in hospitals and running with various fire departments. This was all fine, but right after the slide about the history of paramedics, where they came from and how they came to fill the vital role in emergency medicine they now fill, was an image of degloving. No warning given, just all of a sudden a degloved hand on the screen.

Degloving is a type of injury that usually occurs in factory settings. Somebody's hand gets caught in a machine, and the machine being the cold and calculating monster it is, proceeds to peel off the skin from the muscles and tissues underneath. The hand is flayed alive. It is disgusting to look at a degloving, even if it is projected on a screen and the class came to it cold. Bill felt a rumble in his stomach but was able to swallow it down. Next were images of gunshot wounds and dog bites. There was the image of the man who stepped on a land mine, his legs looked nauseatingly similar to the Italian beef Bill had for lunch. There was the arm of a man who was severely burned by a downed power line. The arm looked less like an arm and more like a hotdog left in a microwave too long. Head injuries, eye injuries, injuries to groins and anuses. Gory and graphic, the instructor named them all with a certain glee as she went through the PowerPoint.

Finally the image of a person's face, or what was left of it, flashed on the screen. A face was all that Bill could remember it as. There was no telling the age, the sex, the gender, or the race of the person. It was mostly just an image of a head where a face should have been. There was the general shape of a head, though pieces seemed to be missing or deformed. Ragged and cut up. But the face was simply gone. Bill's mind tried to fill in where the eyes and nose would have been but whatever was left of the face was an undifferentiated mass of wobbly blood-soaked flesh. It had been torn to ribbons and stacked on itself like a plate of pasta. In the middle of this mound of flesh was a plastic tube. The inorganic item clear and clean against the backdrop of horror. The tube went into what must have once been this person's mouth, came out bent, and disappeared out of the frame.

"What would you call this class?" the instructor asked, pointing to the image. Nobody answered. "Nobody? . . . Well I would call this a . . . win." With a heretofore unused laser pointer she pointed at the place where the tube met the mush. "You see this?" she gave them a second to look. "This, class, is a perfectly placed airway, patent and clean. We could use this airway to bag this guy and get breaths in him. This is good work, class. When you are medics, if you're good, you might be able to do something like this for somebody someday." Bill knew he should sit on his hands, but Bill was the kind of guy who just had to get out what he was thinking. Bill had to talk.

"Did this patient live?" Bill asked without being called on. The instructor looked at Bill, surprised and almost confused.

"Did this person live?" She asked in response to this question. "Did this person live," she said to the class, as if they knew. "Well I'll tell you what, Mr. Um . . ."

"Fence,"

"Well, Mr. Fence," she looked at the picture and then back at Bill. "I sure as hell hope not." She looked again at the image. "That's not our business. What is our business is the medic did a damn fine job placing that airway, damn fine."

That lesson would stick with Bill during his entire career. "Life" in the professional sense for the EMS provider, "life" during the hours they are on the clock, is not life lived, it's not playing with your kids, or cheating on your wife. It's not graduating high school or ending up in jail. Life isn't going to work or getting old, hemorrhoids or football games. Life is perfusion. It is the exchange of chemicals and gasses, sugars and blood, that allow the body to fight off atrophy. That is all that matters in the end. Make sure that perfusion is happening. That O_2 gets in, moves around, and carbon dioxide gets out—pump, flow, repeat. Bill's work life was about perfusion. And perfusion only mattered to Bill up until the point he passed off care for the patient. Should the perfusion stop the moment after the patient was in the care of the hospital staff, it was still a win, so long as he got the patient there and with the chaos of entropy kept at bay. Even if only slightly.

Bill was sitting in the break room when the tones went off at the firehouse. For the first few months of his job it made his blood pump to hear those tones. It meant an opportunity to make an ambulance run, to meet the adventure he was called to meet. The tones beckoned for Bill to get involved in the life of someone else. To risk himself for their sake. It also meant he got to drive the ambulance real fast with lights and sirens, to shoot through traffic and jump across red lights. Maybe wave at the pretty young moms pushing their baby carriages. This excitement wore off over time. Months of picking people off the floor and putting them back in bed while trying to keep from getting their loose stool all over himself kind of dulled the luster.

That said, certain calls could still get his blood pumping. "Wilson Park Fire Department you have an ambulance request. Person down, possibly not breathing at 1210 Morgan Blvd. There is a nurse on the scene." Bill knew the address. He had been called there a hundred times before. The homeowner was a "frequent flier," a person who regularly called for rides to the hospital. This guy called so much that his emergency medical care was practically a line item in the village budget. He suffered from uncontrolled diabetes, a severe heroin addiction, congestive heart failure, COPD, and many, many mental health issues. This call had been a long time coming. The patient lived alone, a visiting nurse as part of a state program would see him once or twice a week, but outside of that his only visitors were bedbugs, EMS crews, his dealer, and night terrors.

There was a bet in the station about when the call would come in that this patient had stopped breathing. Some thought he would go on for years, getting sick, going to the hospital, going to rehab, getting better, getting sick again, and so on. People did live that way. Others assumed the day was just around the corner. Bill had bet it would be the next fall. "Looks like I lost the bet," Bill said to his partner while getting his seat belt on and hitting the ambulance bay garage door.

"Looks that way Billy boy; you owe me a beer after work."

"Yeah my fiancé is gonna hate that. She told me to come straight home after my shift to work on wedding invites. What a bummer." Billy smiled sarcastically, "but a bet's a bet." Bill grabbed the radio. "Ambulance 715 responding to 1201 Morgan." They were off, as fast as they could go. It was only a couple of blocks to the residence; they arrived within three minutes of the call coming in. A young woman in scrubs was standing at the door. She did not look at all concerned as the crew came up with the stretcher, the defibrillator, and a bag of medicines.

"You can slow walk it, I'm pretty sure that guy is dead," the nurse said matter-of-factly as they walked past her into the front room, where the patient did most of his living. The patient was on the couch, exactly where they always found him, obviously dead. His mouth was open, color abnormal, his eyes looked off at nothing. Dead is dead and both Bill and his partner knew it, but they couldn't pay attention to it. There was a dance to be done, a liturgy to perform, and it was best to get on with it.

The house was as the house always was, in total disarray. It was covered in the detritus of a strange, solitary life. There were ashtrays on every free space that didn't have beer bottles, pop cans, or takeout bags on it.

There were two ashtrays that were filled with both cigarette butts as well as discarded needles. He always said they were for insulin but more than a few times they had been used for other substances. The pop cans and beer bottles were also filled with butts and jabs. The ambulance staff knew to be careful when being called to the home as the needles could be anywhere. A paramedic student training with the fire department had leaned on the couch a year previous and was accidentally stuck with a needle that had been absentmindedly left there. She had to get a battery of drugs afterward and was awash in a sea of paperwork. The student left the medic program.

Usually when the nurse was coming the patient cleaned up a little. His greatest fear was that he would end up in a nursing home. He didn't want some visiting nurse claiming he was neglecting himself and getting the state involved in his care. He hadn't cleaned up this time. Not only that but things, and the medics were surprised that they could, had gotten much worse around the house. Bill found a remote and attempted to turn off the TV, which was blaring in the corner of the room. The remote didn't work. Bill's partner walked over to the TV and attempted to turn it off using the buttons on the ancient boxy unit. The buttons didn't work. She found the outlet and unplugged it from the wall, which did the trick. As she did a number of bugs scurried away into the matted carpeting. Garbage bags with sand at the bottom for weight were taped over the windows. The place was dank and damp. Black mold was visibly creeping up the walls. The place stunk of shit and death. Bill used to joke that shit and death smelled like money to a medic. He was rolling in it today.

There were fifteen or so red Solo cups scattered all around the couch. If it had been a frat house the place would have looked like the morning after a toga party, but there had been no party here. The cups were all filled to various levels with a brown substance that could easily have been mistaken for beer if not for the sharp, eye-watering odor of stagnant diseased piss. The patient had obviously become too weak to walk to the bathroom and had taken to peeing in the cups. He had a half-filled sleeve of unused cups laying on the floor next to the couch. The patient had not been able to get off the couch for some time. More than that the dried stain on his pants betrayed the fact that he had gotten too weak even for the cups after a while. Bill used his gloved hands to move the cups away, trying as hard as he could to divorce himself from what he was doing.

"Did you see him die?" Bill shouted over his shoulder at the nurse as he finished clearing a path and made his way over to the body.

"I don't think so. He might have taken a breath but I'm not sure. I took one look at him and called 911. He didn't answer the door so I used the lockbox key and found him there." Bill checked the body for any pulse or signs of breath. The nurse was correct, but the body wasn't putrid or particularly rigid; he wasn't even cold. Since they couldn't be positive when this man took his last breath they had to treat this as an emergency. He could have died seconds before their arrival and therefore have a chance of "coming back."

"Starting CPR," Bill shouted to his partner who began unpacking the defibrillator and getting the electrodes stuck on the body.

The patient was a hairy man, which meant the stickers for the padded electrodes couldn't make direct contact with the flesh due to the mat of hair in the way. Bill's partner slapped the stickers on the hairy chest, pushing them down into the hair as hard as she could. Then she ripped the pads off, an instant waxing. If he had been alive, even in the slightest, this should have elicited a reaction. Nothing. Bill continued with chest compressions while his partner got new electrode stickers on the wires, and attached them to the newly smooth and hairless patches of skin. While all of this was happening the fire engine chase crew arrived on the scene.

By now Bill was dripping with sweat. He had been doing chest compressions for about three minutes straight and it was starting to take its toll on him. Bill was in pretty good shape, but not great shape. He lifted weights four or five times a week, played softball with his buddies on Tuesday nights when he wasn't on shift, and he was an avid fisherman. That was more activity than most firefighters could boast but he didn't do much cardio outside of vomiting after long Friday nights, five minutes of sex twice a week, and the occasional training session at the Fire Department. As such he didn't have all that much gas in the tank and CPR is shockingly demanding on the provider's body.

By this point the patient's ribs had started to crack. Bill could feel the sick sensation of them popping under his hands. With each compression he did more damage to the man's body. On Mondays at the local grocery they sold "cheep" rotisserie chickens, "cheep" meaning half-priced. The special was a favorite of Bill's and his partner's. Each would get their own chicken and a couple of sides. There wasn't all that much white meat on the chicken, but if you really got into the carcass, if you ripped the bones from each other and tore the chest apart, there was a treasure trove of fatty dark meat hiding. The man's ribs felt like tearing into the chicken carcass. The bones and cartilage breaking under his weight. Bill told himself he wasn't there to try and break ribs, he was there to save a life. He just had to do one in order to do the other.

CPR is a terrible intervention, it just happens to be the only intervention in some situations. Chest compressions damage a body horribly, and are rarely effective. About 8 percent of people who receive CPR are alive a month later. That chance of survival goes down dramatically when you add in age and comorbidities, which this patient had in spades. In this case the broken ribs didn't matter all that much as everyone knew he was already dead; that said, even if there was a touch of quickening still left in the man's flesh, CPR would have only delayed the death. CPR also would have made every minute between the start of compressions and the eventual last breath moments of horrible, horrible pain.

"I'm about ready to switch out here," Bill shouted. One of the firefighters lined up behind him. Bill finished the round of compressions he was doing and then passed along the job to the guy behind him. Bill stepped back and caught his breath. Once he had his wind again he looked down at his own chest. His shirt was soaked with what he thought was sweat until he saw its dark red color. "Oh shit," Bill said out loud. He shouldn't have, it was very unprofessional to swear on a call but seeing how there were only firefighters, his partner, a disinterested nurse, and a dead body there, Bill didn't sweat it.

"What is it," one of the new firefighters, full of piss and vinegar, shouted.

"He must have a cut on him somewhere, I just pumped a bunch of his blood right onto my shirt."

"Yup, there it is." Bill's partner pointed out a small skin tear on the patient's arm. Bill quickly grabbed a roll of gauze and covered the wound. Compressions continued while he wrapped. Working together the crew got the body up on the stretcher and out to the ambulance. One of the firefighters, a new guy and just a kid really, hopped in front to drive while Bill and his partner stayed in the back to work on the patient.

By this point Bill had recovered enough to go back to doing chest compressions. He placed his hands in the familiar position above the man's sternum. One hand on top of the other. Palms facing down. And with his strength and his body weight he leaned into the patient, counting out with every compression. The beads of sweat were again pouring from his brow all over the corpse. Dark blood had begun leaking under the bandage and down the arm, pooling on the ambulance floor. What was left of the man's rib cage by this point only vaguely resembled a normal chest. The ribs had been thoroughly mashed to pieces. Most likely the shards of bone had pierced lungs, cut open blood vessels and damaged organs. The dead patient didn't seem to mind.

The ambulance whipped its way through traffic, jumping across red lights. School was getting out down the block and kids were walking on both sides of the road. Most knew to stay away from the flashing lights but some were drawn to that siren song. The new firefighter was all worked up, especially as Bill's partner was screaming at him to both hurry up, drive smoother, slow down. The kid should have heeded the "slow down" in the school zone but his nerves were all pumped up and his foot was heavy. After all they were doing CPR in the back of the cab, this man was a full code and needed to get to the hospital or else he might die. The new kid was the only person on the call who didn't fully understand just how dead the patient was, and nobody had bothered to tell him of the fool's errand they were on. If it wasn't for the reflexes and quick thinking of a crossing guard stopping an excited second grader, they might have had another body to transport that afternoon.

Bill's partner took over compressions as he picked up the cell phone to call into the hospital. They had already transmitted the data from the various monitors they had hooked up to the body when they loaded it into the ambulance. The hospital was well aware that a dead body was rushing toward them, evading various traffic and safety laws. The medical control nurse picked up the phone. Bill rattled off the pertinent information about the patient, including the illnesses he had. Not that the hospital was unaware; they had dealt with this patient often. He told them that the patient had been discovered unresponsive and that CPR had been started. He also told them that the defibrillator, which had been monitoring for heartbeats, had not recommend a shock. Meaning the man did not have the signs of life needed for the electricity to do its work. He didn't say that there was no way the man could be saved, but he didn't have to. Once all the information had been given to the hospital staff, Bill hung up the phone and took back over CPR.

It was another minute or two until the kid pulled the ambulance into the hospital. Having never driven there before, he wasn't sure where the ambulance bay was. He tried pulling up at the front door but the security guard shouted and waved him over to the back of the building where emergency traffic was received. He was lucky neither Bill nor his partner were looking out the front window or else he would have gotten an earful. The kid never made the same mistake again.

When he did arrive at the ambulance bay he was met by a gaggle of doctors, nurses, respiratory therapist, nurse's aides, security, and an uncomfortable chaplain. The kid pulled in, forgetting to turn off the sirens until the doctors screamed at him to do so. He hit a number of buttons before he found the right one. He would catch flak for that one, but later. Right now he was just glad to have pulled the bus in and was ready to wash his hands of the whole thing.

The back doors to the ambulance burst open, and Bill hopped out pulling the stretcher behind him. Once the stretcher was off the ambulance one of the nurse's aides sprung into action performing, extremely ineffective, one-handed chest compressions as Bill pushed the stretcher through the sliding doors and into ER room one: a curtained off room where the most emergent of emergency room patients were taken. More staff members were waiting there, some with smiles on their faces. People love to give CPR; there is an excitement in it. Even if you know how rarely it works, even if you are aware of the damage it does to a body, even if you know the shape the poor person will be in if they should wake up, the TV has done its damage. They still believed, even if they knew it wasn't true, that somehow the person could come back from the dead. That this body could sit up on the table, cough a little, and then look to the doctor and say something along the lines of, "Where are my children?" only to see two towheaded youngsters, overjoyed, central casting stock, in overalls and pastel sweaters, come running from behind the curtain and jump up into their now fully recovered father's arms. Then they turn with wet eyes to the aide who had just finished compressions and say, "Gee thanks for saving my dad, mister."

"All in a day's work son; all in a day's work."

People who do CPR are generally people of action and want those actions to be responsible for saving another's life. That's a noble thing. That's a big part of why Bill got into the game. He wanted to save a life, but he learned to keep another perfusing. Bill walked out of the ER that day seeing the staff still working on his patient. They were starting lines, running tests, and intubating the patient. Bill knew deep down nothing would come of it, but that was a thought he was taught not to think. Bill remembered that destroyed face with the tube in it. An image seared into his brain that would work its way to the front on days like today. He turned to his partner, "Nice run." He found the kid sitting in the break room nervously stirring a cup of coffee.

"Is he gonna make it?" the kid asked. Bill walked up, tussled the kid's hair, gave him a pat on the ass. "I sure as hell hope not buddy." The three walked back to the ambulance to clean up the blood and throw away the wrappers. In the ER, a sheet was being pulled over the face of the corpse. Next of kin were being rudely interrupted at the end of their work day, environmental services had already been paged, room was made at the morgue. The aide who was doing the compressions at the time the death was called was wondering if he had burned enough calories pumping on the man's chest to warrant another slice from the pizza in the back room.

Back at the patient's home the nurse was cleaning up the scene. She wanted it to look presentable for when the family got there. Carefully she picked up piss cup after piss cup. Even though she was wearing two gloves, booties, a mask, safety glasses, a hair cap, and a full length gown she was still terrified of getting the brownish-yellow liquid on herself. She emptied each cup into a pail she found under the sink. Once that was done there were coke cans and used needles to toss, and finally ash trays to empty out.

When she was done the house looked like a pigsty, which was a massive improvement over the hellhole it had been. The nurse was tired now, tired and thirsty. She had no place to go; it was an eight-hour shift she had contracted for and she was paid by the hour. Though the patient was gone and most definitely dead she couldn't leave until she was released. Her boss had already gone home for the day, which meant she could only leave when the family arrived and told her to do so. She needed a drink of water but didn't want to use one of the fifty cups piled high in the sink. That pile had grown for a month or so before it reached critical mass, and then it had sat in the sink for the better part of a year. The nurse opened the fridge and found an unopened water bottle behind a two-liter of coke and a half eaten birthday cake the patient must have bought for himself a week prior when he turned sixty-five.

The nurse grabbed the bottle of water and shut the fridge. As she did she noticed a bright orange piece of paper hanging right there in the middle of the fridge door for all to see. It had obviously been placed on the fridge door so that it would be noticed. On the orange paper in big letters, just above two signatures, one of the patient and the other of his doctor, were written the words "do not resuscitate." The nurse took the paper down and looked at it for a second. She stuck out her lower lip and muttered, "hum," to herself before allowing the paper to fall into the trash. She then pulled the draw string, tied up the bag, and took it out to the garbage. As she did, the patient's family were pulling into the driveway. They thanked her for her work and sent her on her way. Bill, his partner, the kid, the nurse, and the hospital staff, they could all sleep easy that night knowing they did the job they had signed up to do.

Interlude

Incense Rising

Knickknacks and whatnots. Flowers and memorabilia. Pious flags signaling fidelity to that one and only favorite team. Planted at the edges of the sidewalks. Springing up where fences made of orange and salt meet the gravel and the snow. Beneath the viaducts. Hidden. High. In pockets deep and petrified.

In memoriam, they are built: sacred sites to honor the memory of a person, signaling that place where, by bullet or by bus—or by an old buddy driving home from the bar—that person was struck.

Flowers. Umbrellas pooling. Small pocket offerings to place at the foot of a photograph. Smoke. Gestures. Prayers. Incense lifting holy hands. Upward. Upward. To no-one-knows.

Sites such as these saturate the city. They are as much a part of the landscape as subway steps and hurried, flustered, fitted suits. They are special—truly, they are—designated and dedicated and demarcated. And yet, they are but a fraction of the whole. So many others are hidden. In closets. Or in hearts. Or in moments quickly gone. These are simply those that are visible. Those that, built, have the power, for a while, to stay.

Tweakers, junkies, EMTs: all of these are altar-builders, too. Smudgers of sage dipping fingers in fonts, scrawling sacred signs on skin and lips and hearts. Windows stained—or sealed. Blood warmed in golden cups—or oranging leprous on jaundiced walls.

Each injection is a reliquary. Every body broken, a desperate desire. Every invocation born of impotence summoning outlandishly, waiting for Godot, franticly compressing, ribs returned to dust; every lung rejecting the lips of oxygen's violent advance—Ruah returned to the face of the deep—every absence, ache, in pain, a liturgy, screams.

Receiving silence in return.

A famous pastor once described prayer as those with wounded wings attempting to fly.[1] To the abuser, they are deranged. Do the birds not know they are grounded—that I've put them in their place? To those who believe that every flap must lead to flight (and every prayer to a blessing) the birds are clearly wasting breath and time. Your flapping, poor birds, is impractical. It bears no fruits at all. Perhaps it would be better for you to learn how to hunt with your feet planted firmly on the ground.

From their side of the frames that they wear, what the abusers and pragmatists say is true. Nonetheless, spiritual people wear different frames. They know another kind of truth. Not every gesture needs to have an effect. Not every butterfly must create a ripple in a far-off sea. And there's so much more to life than the practical—a spell to cast magic, or prayers, santaclausical, waiting for wished-fors to arrive.

It is true. A rain dance seldom brings rain. And that the resurrection of the dead, no matter how much we confess it, may never actually take place. Just as it's true that hundreds of children marching will not end all oppression and pain. Nonetheless, when firehoses begin to spray and the uniforms engage, striking with dogs and batons—though there is not a *win*, there is something. An unveiling taking place. A revelation for the world to see.

Every altar built, every broken flapping wing, every compression of every chest that's already deceased, every perforation of every vein, every marcher, terrified, marching in hope for the not yet known; every one of these and more is a testimony. A liturgy. A confession that the world as it is, is not as it ought to be. A rededication. And renunciation. My friend is gone. How can this be? We renounce them. We renounce them. We renounce them.

Here in the city, this cry saturates the streets. Yet, only at times can you hear it. Springing up. Along the sidewalks. Near the fences. In the concrete and the snow.

In photographs. In flowers. In incense rising.

In screams.

In screams.

And in the silence received in return.

---

1. "What is insane is not [the bird's] painful, clumsy, efforts to fly, but rather the hand that broke its wings." Alves, *Tomorrow's Child*, 100.

The WAGES of SIN is DEATH. Rom VI.₂₃

Man that is born of a Woman, is of
few days, and full of trouble.
He cometh forth like a flower, and is
cut down; he fleeth also as a shadow, and
continueth not.   Job XIV.1,2.
All flesh is as grass, and all the glory
of Man, as the flower of grass. 1 Pet.I.24.
They spend their days in wealth, and
in a moment go down to the grave. Job XXI.13.
This their way is their folly.
When he dieth, he shall carry nothing away,
his glory shall not descend after him. Psa XLIX.
Verily every Man at his best state
is altogether vanity. Psalm XXXIX.5.
The lofty looks of Man shall be humbled. Isa.II.
It is appointed unto Men once to die, but
after this the Judgment. Heb.IX.27.

Here in the rich, the honour'd, fam'd and great,
See the false scale of happiness complete.
HERE LIES THE GREAT. False Marble! Where
Nothing but poor and sordid Dust lies Here.
REMEMBER DEATH.

Printed for & Sold by Bowles & Carver.   *N. 69 in S.t Pauls Church Yard, London.*

DEATH and LIFE contrasted — or, An ESSAY on MAN.

CHAPTER EIGHT

Walt No More

I guess I'll just lay here, not that there are many other options. The only things I can do is grow hair and nails. Some other stuff is still going on, background stuff. Then again most of it was background stuff. I never knew when my heart was pumping. I never understood the firings of neurons or the exchange of chemicals that kept my body functioning. The act of clawing against entropy we call living. Most of me never rose to the level of consciousness, how little we know and how little what we know matters, or mattered. A lot of that background stuff, the stuff of life, is still working, for now.

I wonder if I'm still Walt? If I'm still I? Who's doing the wondering anyway? It seems I'm still me, a least enough of me that others can look at me and know who I am, for now. That the material that made up my life is still held together enough for the flow that I called "me" to continue to exist, for now. Rust and fire are the same thing moving at different speeds. The wave may have crested but its still together. Not quite consumed by and incorporated back into the ocean from which it sprung. But whatever made me "me" is rusting.

I'm done doing the things I had done to stay together. Running solely on inertia now. There will be no more food or drink. I won't take in oxygen and release carbon dioxide. I'm done with cleaning out the gunk or fixing the broken pieces. I have profused my last profusion. I'll let what remains dilapidate and fade away; I say "let" like I have a choice. Choice is for the living. It's nice to be free of choice. From now on I'm subject to the laws that govern all the unquickened material in the universe. I'm earthly now, part of the heavy bodies. Sinking down for a while but only a while. I'm also sitting on a hospital bed in a nursing home, and it's getting hot in here.

Rust and fire they dance the same dance just in different times. Seems more relevant now as I sit in this bed. Nobody coming for me. The social worker from the nursing home keeps walking in and out of the room. He looks almost angry with me. Like I chose any of this. I heard him on the phone with my nephew in St. Louis. I used to send my nephew Christmas and birthday cards, until he seemed too old for all of that. Didn't make it to his wedding, or his mother's funeral. Now this social worker is leaving the kid messages asking if he can get a funeral home to please come and pick up old Uncle Walt. I don't know if the nephew is gonna do it. I mean it takes a lot of annual ten dollar bills in envelopes to pay for a funeral.

I can't believe that's it. He's the last one to call—my sister's kid who hasn't spoken to me in ages. Must mean the rest of the family is dead or else the social worker can't find them. I wonder what happened to my brother? I have friends I guess they could call, but it's been years since I've seen any of them. I doubt their numbers are in any of my paperwork. I can't remember writing them down. I wonder how they found my nephew, if he is still my nephew. Am I related to anyone anymore? Am I related to everyone and everything? I don't know. It's hot in here.

I'm sure the nursing staff is getting anxious. They had to move my roommate out, but they are going to want to be putting him into bed soon. They usually put him back in bed after dinner, around 5 p.m. or so. Once he's eaten and medicated the guy will sleep all night. Not a problem to anyone. They didn't want him out in the hallway after 5. He would need his meds, but that would make him fall asleep in his chair. Families didn't like to see him leaning over in his wheelchair with spit dripping down his mouth. They wouldn't see him if he was in bed, but the facility also didn't really want to put him back in here with me, being in the state I'm in. Dead bodies are a hard thing to deal with.

The social worker is trying his best, probably getting a lot of heat from above and below. I've become a problem. Not worth much to anyone anymore. I can no longer produce. Being no longer productive, I am now the product. What remains, I am remains. Remains. How can I be an "I" if that "I" is plural? Nobody wants what remains. Nobody wants to deal with what remains. Hence the expense of paying the funeral parlor to deal with me or the "mes" that now remains. It gets confusing, and it's not cheap to have professionals handle what remains. They gouge families, preying on their grief, making what they can from their sorrow. They aren't bad people, they just live in a society where people pay for their services, and they will charge whatever it is those people are willing to pay. This can be a lot.

What happens to me? With nobody willing to pay to see me disposed of? It used to be that Medicaid, on which I've been for the past few years, helped. The program that has paid for me to be fed, clothed, and housed here in this facility used to kick in some money for the remains. They used to pay a pittance to the funeral parlors willing to do the paperwork to have a body burned and buried or else dumped in a potter's field for the worms to deal with the remains. But some years ago a politician asked, "Why should the taxpayer deal with the remains?" Why was it society's problem to help with the disposal of the remains? Remains don't vote, or at least they aren't supposed to. Since they don't vote they certainly don't need some fancy funeral on the government's dime. Such a thing seems excessive and wasteful. Cutting funding for funerals was an easy enough cut to make from the budget. A line item to be taken out with only the howls of ghosts to complain.

Here I lay, no society to bail me out. No government fund to assist the social worker in dealing with what remains. What happens to me now? I can't just lay here in this hospital bed to rot. What would my roommate do? What of the smell? Certainly the health inspector doesn't want a corpse moldering in some nursing home room. The politicians who took the money out of the budget probably have life insurance policies that come free with their jobs. They probably belong to families who can help pay for the funeral. Maybe they have a nice grassy plot in a well-appointed cemetery somewhere. A mausoleum where the family all takes their final rest. The politicians certainly believe there is a process for what remains, something in existence that can handle the problem I have become. They must think there is a cooler somewhere at the bottom of the building. Drawers built in the walls like in the movies. My body can be slid in there and left to wait for some relative to show up and foot the bill.

The only cooler in this building is full of tonight's dinner. I don't think anyone wants me in there next to the Salisbury steak. There is a bigger cooler downtown at the coroner's office that I could be taken to. But who is gonna come out and grab me. The coroner doesn't have a meat wagon running all around the city picking up the old and in the way. Imagine the cost of that to the taxpayers. Even if they did, how big a cooler do the politicians think they have? They need room for the murder victims, the bodies of people who are found in the street with huge gashes on their heads. The coroner needs space for the strange deaths. The accidents and incidents. The sudden and shocking. They need room for the illnesses that don't make any sense, not an old man whose death anyone could have seen coming.

The coroner only deals with 3 or 4 percent of the bodies that flood these streets and that is what they have storage for. If you put every body without a next of kin, every person who died without a family member willing to pick up the insane tab of a modern funeral, everybody who died without a plan or a person to make a plan for them—if you had room for all of those remains, well we would need a football field of fridge space. You'd need as much cold storage as an Amazon Fulfillment Center. And my nephew isn't gonna pay to keep old "had been" Walt here on ice. What the politicians who took away the Medicaid money don't know is that for those of us who didn't fit in the living world, there isn't a place for us among the dead. But like I said before, fire and rust are the same thing. I am a problem that will go away, eventually.

The social worker is back now. I think the nephew may have given in. He has my chart in hand and is reading something off it over the phone. My Social Security number, at least that is still mine even after death. That is more permanent than thought, or vision, or mass or strength. At least my remains still have a Social if nothing else. How long that lasts I don't know. There is money involved so it could be a while. I no longer have rights, I no longer have worth, only cost. What remains is negation. Who I am is now what I owe, or what someone owes on my behalf—which appears to be around $1,500.

"That's right, they will pick him up and do a direct cremation for fifteen hundred. Hold on please sir I'm gonna put you on speakerphone while I look through some of these documents." The social worker hits the speaker button and throws the phone on my bed next to me. It bounced and hit my leg; he didn't say sorry. Then he starts leafing through my paperwork, some he brought from the office, some comes from the drawer next to my bed. The EMTs brought it with me when I was transferred from the hospital. I was out of it then. If the social worker had asked me when I was alive where my paperwork was I couldn't have told him.

"Yeah, it doesn't say anything in his paperwork about a life insurance policy." The social worker spoke loudly, rolling his eyes and ruffling papers. I couldn't tell if he was actually looking at them or just making noise for effect.

"I know Uncle Walt was in the Navy. Mom used to talk about it all the time. I guess Grandma was really nervous when he was away, she used to light a candle for him at mass."

"He may well have been, it's just not here in his paperwork. If I were you I would contact the VA. They should have a file on him. If he does qualify for burial benefits they should pay you back for the cremation."

"Can I call them now and get the money up front?" My nephew sounds older; he sounds a little upset. I wonder if it's my death bothering him or the fact that he just got a call from a stranger in the middle of the workday, telling him his near-forgotten uncle's remains need to be dealt with and that the only person left to deal with them is him. Largely because I put his phone number on a form years ago without ever really thinking about it. Could go either way, really.

"No sir I'm sorry but we don't have time for that. It is our policy here at Waterfall Oaks [there was neither a waterfall nor an oak for miles around] that all remains of expired patients are to be removed within three hours of a death. We are already on hour six." The social worker is looking at his watch now. He has to go home, his shift ends at 5 p.m. and there isn't another social worker until the morning. No way the boss is gonna let him go with me here. Doesn't matter to me though, I guess I'm "expired" and you can leave out expired things all you want; expired is binary. You either are or you aren't and once you are expired, well, you can't really expire anymore can you?

"I'm sorry I know you have a job to do. It's just that's a lot of money and I haven't seen Walt in like a decade." Try fifteen years.

"Like I said, sir, you can get the money back from the VA."

"Maybe I can but how long is that gonna take? I have rent to make at the end of the month, I have bills to pay and kids to feed." Wonder when he had kids. "I might get the money back some day but what am I supposed to do until then?"

"I don't know, sir, but something has to be done now about this body and you are the only relative we can find. Do you know if there is anybody else we could call?" The social worker is tossing papers around the room now. He's pissed. I've seen him like this before when residents act up. For a social worker the guy has a hard time controlling his emotions. That said, I guess I should have taken care of this burial stuff before I died. Well tough for him the expired may not have rights, but we also don't have worries.

"No, not on Uncle Walt's side, unless he had some family I don't know about. His brother died ages ago and mom's been gone five years now." Wow five years ago my baby sister bit it. I wonder how expiration is going for her. Do I get to see her now or something? If she were to show up here I'm guessing she would be all sorts of pissed with me for laying this on her oldest boy's shoulders. I don't blame her but the kid has money. At least last time I heard he was doing well for himself, maybe that was just his mother bragging. Still I'm sure he can swing a measly fifteen hundred dollars to deal with his dear uncle's remains, or is it the remains of his uncle? Either way.

"So what does the fifteen hundred get me again?" What does it get him? What does it get me is the real question.

"Well it pays for what's known as a direct cremation. That means the funeral home will come here to pick up the body. They will then perform the cremation and the cremains will be placed in a box." Oh they call it "cremains." That's cute. "I think you have to come and pick them up; I'm not sure. The funeral home will tell you about that later."

"Come and pick them up? I live ten hours away, come on."

"I know it's frustrating sir, again I'm not sure what they do with the cremains. Maybe they'll send them to you."

"Oh no, you aren't gonna send the ashes of some forgotten relative here." Who is that voice in the background?

"I'm sorry, that was my wife, she is a little leery about death and dead bodies and all of that."

"I don't blame her sir." I think the social worker does blame her. "Look again I don't really know how it all works, they will communicate with you about that. Now like I said I just need you to pick a cremation provider."

"I don't know anybody who does that work. When I was a kid the family always used Johnson's Funeral Home, is that still around? I haven't been back since mom's funeral, of all things."

"Yes Johnson's is still around, but it was bought out by Zeus Cooperation."

"What's Zeus Cooperation?"

"I think their main business is corporate litigation and small appliance repair, but they also buy up old mom and pop funeral homes, keep the names, and jack up the prices. If you wanted a direct cremation from Johnson's it would cost probably $4,000."

"My God, $4,000 just to burn up a body?"

"Well $3,500 anyway. No if I were you I'd go with Eternal Flames Cremation Company, or else The Cheap Cremation Company. I'll text you their numbers." Look at the social worker dig through his pile of papers, like a needle in the haystack. Oh look, he found the sheet. "Huh, would you look at that, Eternal Flames and The Cheap Cremation Company both have the same number." That social worker can text with the best of them, holding the paper in one hand while his thumb works away on the other. "Anyway, I just texted it to you. Did you get it?"

"Yeah, I got it." I can hear yelling in the background. Didn't he invite me to his wedding? I should have gone to his wedding. If I did I bet his wife wouldn't be so upset. I know I had something else to do that day but no idea what. We never know what is gonna come back to bite us. I guess I died before it really came back around. Still should have gone.

"Um, well," the nephew sounds like he is wavering. "You're gonna have to give me a minute to talk this over with my wife. This is a lot of money just to be laying out."

"I know, sir, but again you should be able to get the money back."

"That's if he was in the military."

"He was, wasn't he?"

"That's what I was told but you never know." I was in the military, of course I never told him I was only in for a year and my discharge wasn't what you would call honorable. Still, hopefully the VA will help him out, they never did me any favors I can tell you that much.

"Well, let's hope so, please call me back as soon as you know which funeral home you are going to go with so I can get the paperwork in order. The management is getting very antsy about this."

"Okay sir I'll let you know as soon as we make a choice." I don't know what the choice is. It has to do something with me. The social worker is pissed; he threw his phone down again. This time right into my leg. If I was alive, if I was still clawing back against the chaos, I would have hollered. Who knows why the living holler? It doesn't change the pain they are feeling. But I would have. He knows it too.

"Sorry." Well that's nice, he is talking to a dead body. If he really was sorry he wouldn't have farted when he was picking up his papers like he was in a room all by himself. It's funny to watch the social worker walk out into the hallway, checking his watch as he goes. I know he doesn't want to be alone in this room with me, but he also doesn't want to be out there with all the other problems. I pose a single issue, one that, once solved, is over. The living, they remain more complicated. Their problems build up and change. They grow and swell. They can be loud or sad or dirty or smelly. I can only be dirty or smelly. I'm not going to get any dirtier for a while, but I know he's worried about the smell. Which is silly really, it's not like I'm just gonna turn any time soon. Though I have to admit it's hot in this room. I guess no sense running the AC for a corpse.

I'll lay here for a while in the heat; don't mind me. Growing nails, firing synapses, shedding skin, saying my final goodbyes to dying cells. I can wait for as long as anyone. No real rush on my end. Still, every couple of minutes the social worker pops his head in the door, hoping I guess that I had gotten up and walked away while he was back in the office grabbing a cup of coffee or else sitting on the john hoping none of the other staff would notice he was there after his shift ended. Oh, here he is again, on the phone. I wonder if he's talking to my nephew?

"Honey, I'll be home as soon as I can get home." Unless he and my nephew got real close real quick I'm guessing he's talking to someone else. "What do you want me to do? Shove the corpse on the street corner and hope that the sanitation department comes along and grabs it?" He is quiet for a while. I guess his wife had plans for the night and I'm throwing a wrench in them. "I'm really sorry, but you are going to have to tell your sister to wait. It shouldn't be that much longer, his nephew is working on it now." Silence again. "No, there is nobody I can call. That's not how it works." There's a long pause. He must be getting the business. "I know, I know, but I need this job. Look, honey, I told you before. . . . Yes, I'm sorry, I won't 'honey' you. Look, Barbara, there is no management here after 5 p.m. The nurse will not take care of it. The aides have their own work to do. This is on me to get sorted out. I promise I'm on it and doing the best I can, but these people are going to take time to make a decision. I will be home as soon as I possibly can. . . . Well you don't need to be cruel. Maybe I should have gone into business with my dad, but this is the life I, no we, chose. I'm sorry it's not up to your mother's standards. We can't all be life insurance salesmen." He's getting pissed now. "No, no, it's okay Barb. It happens. You have every right to be frustrated. I'm frustrated. They don't pay me enough for this bullshit. Look, why don't you just go ahead and I'll meet you at the restaurant." He's sitting down on the corner of the bed now; how informal. "I know, I know, but I'm gonna have to shower anyway. I am literally currently sitting on the corner of a dead man's bed, and his body is still in the bed. I'm gonna have to shower."

I wonder why he has to shower after sitting on the corner of my bed? I've been cleaned up. The staff changed my diaper. They even gave me a bed bath for some reason. They changed out the linens. I might be the cleanest I've been since I came to this place. This guy, I've seen him in his office eating a sandwich after shaking Jerry's hand. Jerry had that hand down his pants all day and this guy didn't so much as Purell afterward. Now he is going to have to shower after sitting on the corner of a bed with clean sheets and a lump of slowly separating molecules sitting in the middle. His fridge is full of dead things. I bet he has a fruit basket on the counter in his apartment loaded to the brim with a cornucopia of decaying produce. What makes me so bad compared with all of that? Throw in a dead body and everyone gets so superstitious. What does he need to wash off? Even when he does get in the shower he is going to wash his own dead skin down the drain. There isn't all that much difference between me and him. Fire and rust are the same process. Oh, the phone's ringing.

"Hello, yes sir, were you able to talk with the funeral home?" Oh good, he put the phone on speaker again. He is one of those types that likes to hold the phone out in front of him and kind of shout at it.

"Well, yes, we did call the what was it again, the cheap one?" Oh great, probably gonna burn me with like ten other people. My ashes will get mixed with the charred remains of some dude's small intestines. What's left of my nose mixed with someone's backside.

"The Cheap Cremation Company."

"Yeah, that's it. So I guess they are going to come and pick up my uncle's . . . what do you call it . . . carcass." Pretty sure that's not what you call it nephew.

"I think 'remains' is what they say sir. Okay, did they say how long it would be?"

"Well I told them that he was in the nursing home and no family was there." The social worker may have only mouthed "damn it" but I swear even with dead ears I could hear it. "I guess he had another pick up first so it should be an hour or two." The social worker threw the phone on my leg again. I wonder if you can bruise after death? Mr. Zen then takes a few deep breaths, classic social work.

"Okay very good, look sir I want to again tell you I'm truly sorry for your loss, and I'm sorry for having to call you out of the blue and ask for your help with this. It really is a kind thing you did for your uncle." Would have been kind of him to come here and visit when I was alive.

"It's the least I could do." Oh there goes his wife in the background again. I guess she thinks it was a little more than the least that he could do. The social worker doesn't look too comfortable listening to someone else getting dressed down by their wife. I guess it is a portent of things to come for him. I might have felt bad for both of these men a few hours ago. But as it turns out your concern for the individual drifts away pretty quickly. I'm slowly no longer an "I" at all. I'm on my way to or back to something larger, something deeper. The individual just doesn't seem to matter as much now as it used to. The problems of a single person just don't amount to a hill of beans. I used to worry so much about bothering other people, about getting in the way. Now let them deal with me, let them have to pick me up and carry me around. Let them stoke the flames, or not, I really don't care, or at least care less and less by the moment.

Still, it's hot in this room. I hope the cremation guy hurries up. I don't want to lie in bed forever. Though I guess I'm not just lying in bed anymore. I'm leaking off, parts of me or what was me, are breaking apart to go on their own way. Atoms being shed. Cells breaking down into smaller pieces and those pieces melting away. Nothing to organize it all anymore. Pieces of me are simply pieces now, no me to hold on to them. Me, whatever sticky stuff that is or was, or is becoming, is ceasing to be a thing at all. All that is left is experience. The experiences of a trillion, trillion atoms that used to be one thing. One voice now a symphony.

When there was an I, whenever that was, I knew this feeling of being picked up. It was one of the oldest feelings I had. Being picked up by mom and dad, being carried around the room. Taken to where I ate and where I slept. Walked and bounced. Held over a shoulder and burped. I knew what it was like to be lifted and moved, forced to go where someone else wanted me to go. Helpless now as I fade; helpless then as I was coalescing from the ether of unconsciousness. We return from whence we came, I guess. Rust being the same as fire. Mom and Dad were never this rough when they lifted me, at least not often. Even if they were there was a feeling in their lifting me up. If it was harsh there was anger, if it was gentle then care. These hands that lift the body, what's still holding together anyway, out of the bed—these hands, they are indifferent. They are the hands of the worker who has a task to do. That task brings in money. It is not an end in itself. These hands do not lift me out of care; they lift to get paid. They are not cruel or kind, simply efficient.

I guess I'm away from home now. Not that it was ever home. In fact home seems like everywhere I am at this point. There is no real differentiation, just movement. I belong everywhere but a home is nowhere to be found. I'm less and I'm more and I'm in a room. Oh it's hot in here, way hotter than in the nursing home, but I care so much less. Or don't care at all. I guess this is it. Rust and fire are the same but fire works quicker. Things are speeding up now. The "I" erodes, and melts, and is gone. One becomes billions and the billions, while gathered together, no longer have anything to do with the other beyond proximity. What will the future of the billions be? What will their, our, futures be?

This pile will sit on a shelf until it's time to get rid of it. The funeral director will look at the box taking up her precious storage space with ire. She will make calls to the nephew who at first will express apologies, give dates, not follow through. Eventually the calls won't be answered or returned. One day, when someone thinks it's been long enough, what remains will be unceremoniously disposed of. Dumped down a drain or scattered out in the back, along with all the other forgotten boxes. I don't worry about it because "I" am no longer. It would always be this way, rust and fire being equal. But if an "I" remained at all, maybe tucked in one of these atoms here. Maybe it wouldn't want to rust or burn. I don't know.

Bibliography

Alves, Rubem. *The Poet, The Warrior, The Prophet*. London: SCM, 2002.

———. *A Theology of Human Hope*. St. Meinard, IN: Abbey, 1975.

———. *Tomorrow's Child: Imagination, Creativity, and the Rebirth of Culture*. Eugene, OR: Wipf & Stock, 2009.

———. *Transparencies of Eternity*. Translated by Jovelino Ramos and Joan Ramos. Series Sapientia. Miami: Convivium, 2010.

Bloch, Ernst. *The Principle of Hope*. 3 vols. Translated by Neville Plaice et al. Cambridge: MIT Press, 1995.

Camus, Albert. *The Myth of Sisyphus*. New York: Knopf Doubleday, 2018. https://www.google.com/books/edition/The_Myth_of_Sisyphus/XmpoDwAAQBAJ?hl=en&gbpv=0&bshm=rime/1.

Francis of Assisi. "The Canticle of the Creatures." In *Francis of Assisi: Early Documents*, edited by Regis J. Armstrong, J. A. Wayne Hellmann, and William Short, 113–14. New York: New City, 1999.

Franz, Koun. "Buddhism's 'Five Remembrances' Are Wake-Up Calls for Us All." Lion's Roar: Buddhist Wisdom for Our Time, March 30, 2021. https://www.lionsroar.com/buddhisms-five-remembrances-are-wake-up-calls-for-us-all/.

Puleo, Mev. "Rubem Alves." In *The Struggle Is One: Voices and Visions of Liberation*, 185–204. Albany: State University of New York Press, 1994.

Shi, Kaida. *Who's Who III*. Zhoushan: Zhejiang Ocean University: 2020.

Townes, Emilie M. *Womanist Ethics and the Cultural Production of Evil*. New York: Palgrave Macmillan, 2006.

Tillich, Paul. *Dynamics of Faith*. World Perspectives 10. New York: Harper, 1957.

Westhelle, Vítor. *The Church Event: Call and Challenge of a Church Protestant*. Minneapolis: Fortress, 2010.

———. *Eschatology and Space: The Lost Dimension in Theology Past and Present*. New York: Palgrave Macmillan, 2012.

———. "Scientific Sight and Embodied Knowledges: Social Circumstances in Science and Theology." *Modern Theology* 11.3 (1995) 341–61. https://doi.org/10.1111/j.1468-0025.1995.tb00070.x.

Žižek, Slavoj, dir. *The Pervert's Guide to Ideology*. New York: Zeitgeist Films, 2012.